With tenacity, tenderness and humor Peter Rosenberger brings hope to those who find themselves in the overwhelming and sometimes lonely role of caregiver.

Amy Grant

As caregivers, we often feel isolated, but for me, reading and listening to Peter feels like a one-on-one encounter. It could be as intensely personal to you, too!

Graham Kerr, former Galloping Gourmet

Written by one who has "been there and done that," Peter Rosenberger offers caregivers practical advice for everyday living, perspective on their role and relationships, and hope grounded in Christian faith and fellowship. This book is an important resource for caregivers—and for those who care for the caregivers.

Kenneth L. Farmer, Jr., MD
Major General, US Army (Retired),
Former Commanding General, Walter Reed Army Medical Center
and North Atlantic Regional Medical Command

None of us ever plan to be in a position like Peter, but it happens. This book provides help and sign posts for the caregiver! When I was helping to care for a stroke-ridden father for many years, I wish I had had this book to lean upon!

Joe Bonsall, The Oak Ridge Boys

Not only is this a great tool for providing care for another, its spiritual principles are applicable to any situation that challenges us in life. I LOVE the solution of GPS (Grace, Purpose, Stewardship) for navigating the FOG (Fear, Obligation, Guilt) that caregivers experience.

Elizabeth Moss, LPN
CEO, Caregivers By Wholecare

Peter Rosenberger is absolutely amazing. A true leader by example. Hear what he has to say and you will understand why he is the most qualified person to teach you how to thrive as a caregiver.

David Asarnow, CEO Business Oxygen, Inc.

In a world hung up on trying to make sense out of hard times, Peter drives the point home that "We don't have to understand—God understands, and that's enough. He is enough—He is always enough." Peter leads readers through such painful situations with humor and practical help—and in the process, our faith is strengthened. This is THE book for caregivers, written by one with scars and immense credibility.

Jeff Foxworthy

Peter has "walked the walk" as a caregiver and with humility has birthed, I believe, a divinely inspired perspective for a new generation of caregivers. As a caregiver myself, I have experienced the isolation component that Peter addresses in this book. As you read ahead, you will meet an "understanding friend" who will introduce you to ways that can help you rise above your circumstances.

Marianne Clarke, EdD, Caregiver

Peter is authentic in his understanding and awareness when he writes about caregiving—he knows the journey intimately. He is also theologically wise in the midst . . . when he says "we are stewards not owners."

Keith G. Meador, MD, ThM, MPH
Professor of Psychiatry and Health Policy Director,
Center for Biomedical Ethics and Society Associate Dean,
Student Health and Wellness Vanderbilt University

H pe
for the
Caregiver

Encouraging Words to
Strengthen Your Spirit

PETER ROSENBERGER

WORTHY
Inspired

Published by Worthy Inspired, an imprint of Worthy Publishing Group, a division of Worthy Media, Inc. One Franklin Park, 6100 Tower Circle, Suite 210, Franklin, TN 37067.

WORTHY is a registered trademark of Worthy Media, Inc.

HELPING PEOPLE EXPERIENCE THE HEART OF GOD

Cover Design by Jeffery Jansen / Aesthetic Soup
Page Layout by Bart Dawson

Printed in the United States of America

2 3 4 5—LBM—19 18 17 16

Solus Christus

The ultimate caregiver of a wounded bride.

CONTENTS

Part III: Lifestyle

Part IV: Planning

FOREWORD
by Ken Tada

Millions of caregivers are out there plodding through mundane routines with hardly the strength to look up, let alone read a book. So why read this one? Especially a book that reminds them of their never-altering, daily responsibilities?

Count me in that group. For more than thirty-two years of marriage, I have been helping my wife who is a quadriplegic. Sure, several of Joni's friends help, but the main job falls on me, her husband. So of all the books I might read in my free time, why read this one?

Because I need to. I was convinced of that after reading only the first chapter. *Hope for the Caregiver* is not a fancy title, but it delivers on its promise. You and I need hope that we can make it, hope that we won't throw in the towel or walk away from our wedding vows. We need to know why we do this crazy 24/7 routine, why we take thirty minutes to order four different kinds of pills over the phone, making sure the pharmacist gets it right. We need to know how much that counts in the long run. Finally, we need to know that a greater source of strength is waiting to pour Himself into our weary minds, hearts, and bodies.

My wife and I are involved in Joni and Friends, a worldwide ministry that serves special-needs families in the love of Jesus. We meet so many couples who tell us they simply couldn't make it without their faith in God. But often, in the middle of the night when you get up to turn your spouse, it can feel like He's not there. Well, He is. And sometimes we need to be reminded that God *is* the source of our strength.

Besides, I like listening to Peter Rosenberger. Joni and I have known Peter and his wife Gracie for many years. I won't go into the details about her disability (or I should say, disabilities), but we don't hold a candle to the challenges the Rosenbergers face. Yes, caring for my quadriplegic wife has its difficulties—especially adding her chronic pain to the mix—but our circumstances have never seemed as grim as Peter's and Gracie's. But that's for him to tell in this book.

Plus, *Hope for the Caregiver* is easy to read. The chapters are short, and you can, with no trouble, read a few pages and then come back to it after running to the drugstore. Peter has taken great pains to make everything practical. Are your medical bills piling up? Is your insurance not covering everything it should? Are you wondering if you should switch doctors? Peter's got helpful advice for you—stuff you can really do something about.

I felt like Peter was speaking to me in this book. Sometimes it helps knowing that you're not alone, that others have charted the confusing labyrinth of medical and family issues. It helps to know that you're not the only one who would really rather go out to the backyard and enjoy a cigar than spend the evening ferreting through EOBs.

This book is worth your time because three decades of caregiving has earned Peter a certain degree of authority. I mean, the guy has been through hell, yet he tells his caregiver story with humor, inspiration, and down-to-earth wisdom. Most of all, it's worth your time because (how can I say this as a husband, as a man) *we all need help*. I don't like asking for help, but that doesn't mean I don't need it. And you need it, too.

Gracie Rosenberger and my wife Joni are true treasures. They are unique and gifted women who have contributed much to Peter's life and mine, and we love them. They are our wives, and we expect to stand by their sides "until death do us part." I suspect that you truly love your spouse, your child, your parent(s), your brother, your sister, your friend. You wouldn't be hanging in there and holding onto these pages if you did not value your relationship with the special person in your life who lives with challenges.

So when it comes to books on caregiving, is there really anything new under the sun? I think there is, and you're holding it in your hands. I hope I've convinced you that this short but powerful collection of essays from my friend Peter contains fresh insights for you. So try it out. Take it to your loved one's next medical appointment and peruse it in the waiting room. Who knows? By the time the appointment is over, your heart may sense something it hasn't felt in a long time: a new resolve to keep caring and giving, not so much out of duty but out of a fresh wind of love.

Ken Tada

Joni and Friends International Disability Center

Fall 2014

———

The teaching of the wise is a fountain of life.

Proverbs 13:14

INTRODUCTION

E ach Wednesday morning, I attend a men's Bible study at my church. With the usual half-dozen men meeting over coffee, we work through Scripture, as well as various theological books. We share burdens, successes, funny stories, and even tragic losses. One morning, I opened a discussion about prayer and admitted that I don't often know how to pray for Gracie or myself.

"What do I even ask for?" I blurted out while holding my hands up helplessly. "If she's in a lot of pain, do I ask God for pain relief, or should I go 'all-in' and ask Him for a total body healing—including legs?"

I mean, we are praying to the King of kings, Lord of lords, Alpha and Omega, the Great I AM. Why do we dance around the subject of prayer? Sometimes it seems that many try to wash God's hands and "clean up the mess." It's unsettling to realize that God is not as freaked out about our suffering as we are. Going further, He deliberately allows.

Some folks may take issue with that statement, and want to put it back on the afflicted. "There must be some sin blocking God's provision," is a common statement. If, as in my family's case, amputated limbs are a sign of God's displeasure at sin(s), then there would be a whole lot more amputees in this world, and in pulpits.

God's use of suffering in our lives—without an expiration date on this earth—doesn't sell well. Imagine going to a crusade to hear big-time evangelists preach that message! That's why you hear words like *victory*, *breakthrough*, and *blessings* instead of *perseverance*, *endurance*, and *resolve*. People want to be bailed out of their misery, and, to be blunt, who can blame them?

That plays for a while, but eventually one has to stop praying for a bailout and start living a life of faith and trust—and our prayers change.

As I pondered on how to pray, and what to pray specifically as a caregiver, I wrote the Caregiver's Prayer. My hope is that it will serve as a helpful road map to a more meaningful prayer life for my fellow caregivers.

THE CAREGIVER'S PRAYER

Heavenly Father, I love _____.
I have committed my life to caring for him/her,
Yet I know the task is greater than my abilities.

As I seek to help another,
I ask for strength to shoulder the burdens before me.
Yet I also ask for the wisdom to know what is mine to carry.

I ask for the courage to admit my failures and make amends.
I thank You for Your grace and mercy,
and ask that You help me daily apply it to myself
and extend it to others.

As I walk through this long valley of the shadow of death,
I ask for a deeper awareness of Your presence to calm my fears.
As I glance backwards, may I only see Your provision.
As I look forward, may my eyes see Your guidance.

May I reflect You as I minister to this one whom I love.
I pray all this in the name of Your Son, Jesus Christ,
Who laid down His own life . . . for me.

PART I

❧

HEAD

Happy is the man who finds wisdom,
and the man who gains understanding.

Proverbs 3:13 NKJV

Tomorrow hopes we learned
something from yesterday.

John Wayne

I do believe I'm feelin' stronger every day.

Chicago, Peter Cetera/James Pankow

———◦◦———

I'll never be your beast of burden
My back is broad but it's a hurting.

The Rolling Stones, Mick Jagger/Keith Richards

———◦◦———

I can't carry it for you . . . but I can carry you!

Samwise to Frodo, Lord of the Rings

Chapter 1

❖

SHOCK AND AWE

When I am afraid, I will trust in You.

Psalm 56:3 HCSB

As caregivers, we sometimes experience "flash-bulb moments" so shocking that the memory is seared into our brains for a lifetime. One of mine came at St. Thomas Hospital more than twenty-five years ago—at 3:00 a.m.

Memories intensify with the engagement of all five senses, and that night, each of mine felt slammed. The bitter taste of old coffee filled my mouth as I hunched over a stack of medical records, while I fought against gagging from the nauseating stench of my wife's fresh vomit still on my clothes. Caffeine and stress fought against me as I tried in vain to steady my shaking hands and calm my heart down after watching her endure a seizure. Ignoring the looks of nurses and staff, as well as the beeps of countless machines and various announcements over the hospital's intercom system, I sat halfway down the dimly lit ward with my back against the wall and scanned over charts, lab reports, and doctors' notes in the massive folder that bore my wife's name.

Despite three years of marriage, that night served as my first opportunity to review the file that had steadily grown since Gracie's car accident at age seventeen, on November 18, 1983.

After her wreck and lengthy recovery, Gracie returned to Nashville's Belmont University where I first met her. Mutual friends felt us a perfect match, and, from the moment I first saw her, I agreed.

"Peter, she's wonderful, but you need to know that she had a serious car accident that left her permanently hurt," one of Gracie's friends warned.

Several others, including her family, repeated the admonition as our relationship grew, but with no frame of reference as to what the caution meant, I plunged ahead.

Nodding my head with an understanding I lacked, I assumed that no matter what her injuries, I still wanted to meet her. My limited understanding led me to think, *How bad could the car wreck have been? After all, she's back at school, and others were trying to set us up.*

As she walked toward me, I swear to you that the sun followed her every step. Although noticing the limp, it didn't detract. This girl was beautiful in ways that I could not express. A nearby friend offered a squeegee to help with the drool flowing from my open mouth as I watched her head my way. Surprising me with her forthrightness, she walked right up to me, stuck out her hand, smiled, and said, "Hi Peter, I'm Gracie Parker. I need to sit down. May I put my feet in your lap?"

Plopping her misshapen feet into my lap, we sat with a group of friends in the courtyard by the student center. Noticing the scars extending above the ankles and disappearing under her cropped jeans, I "smoothly" blurted out, "Good Lord, girl, what happened to you?!"

With a direct look, her frank but understated remark was only, "I had a bad car accident."

———⋙⋘———

A whirlwind courtship and three years of marriage later, I sat outside a hospital room in the middle of the night, following my wife's grand mal seizure. This time, I directed the same question to the pile of medical documents in front of me.

*"Good Lord, girl, what **happened** to you?"*

Not even her family had read what I now studied. Poring through doctors' notes, I realized Gracie's accident was unlike anything I imagined. This was no fender-bender resulting in a broken limb that would simply serve as a weather indicator for life. Turning the pages, one word just kept flooding my mind: *devastation*.

Tears hit a few of the pages, as I hung my head in grief and hopelessness. For the first time in my life, I felt a despair that would hover over me for the next dozen years—and one that still requires my vigilance to guard against.

Reading until dawn, I closed the massive folder and sadly noted that the cover stated, "Volume 4 of 4." Before converting most of her records electronically years ago, the volumes grew to seven—for just one of the twelve hospitals where she's received treatment.

The events of that night forever altered me, along with the way I view life, hospitals, doctors, other people, my wife, and even God. Although immature, I was devoted. My sincere desire to care for this extraordinary woman led me to begin this journey. I never imagined, however, that the road would contain such suffering, loss, heartache, self-sacrifice, failure, and love.

My love for Gracie committed me to an existence dominated by constant brutal realities that would end with a funeral, but hopefully not mine. While my dying would remove me from the daily burden of caring, my death would also create an even greater hardship for the ones I loved most. So even"driving off a bridge" represented a poor option. That night in the hospital corridor, my heart sunk as I stared at a future full of relentless challenges with no expiration date.

I felt trapped, but also understood the need for me to stay alive and healthy.

A difficult place for a twenty-six-year-old man.

A difficult place for a fifty-two-year-old man.

To date, Gracie's journey includes at least seventy-eight operations (that I can count), multiple amputations (not just both legs, but multiple revisions on both legs), treatment by more than sixty physicians in a dozen hospitals, seven different insurance companies, and medical costs cresting nine million dollars.

As her sole caregiver for nearly thirty years, I often recall that shock-and-awe moment in that lonely hospital when I read her chart for the first time. Somehow pushing the massive despair into an emotional box, I threw myself into the task of fixing that which cannot be fixed, and managing that which cannot be managed.

My wife, my responsibility.

———※———

Someone once asked, "If possible, what would you say to your younger self?"

This book is the answer to that question.

On these pages, I've condensed a lifetime of experience into what I hope will be a lifeline of help to my fellow caregivers. These pages contain the things I wish someone had communicated to me.

Through it all, I've learned quite a bit about America's healthcare system. Through marriage to someone with extreme pain, disability, and chronic crises, I've learned even more about perseverance, love, and relationships.

It's not easy caring for a suffering human being—one who lives with a severe disability and intractable pain. I often tell my wife, "You're easy to love, but you're hard to love well."

Armed only with a relentless persistence, a goofy sense of humor, a few "smarts," and a degree in music (composition, *piano principal*), I somehow keep the plates spinning. When it comes to "wanna-be" stand-up comedians who play the piano and take care of a disabled wife for decades, I'm the best there is.

Others may offer opinions about caregivers—seems a lot of folks are talking about this subject. That's okay; everyone is entitled to an opinion. On the subject of "how to help a caregiver," however, my experience trumps opinion.

> Blessed are the flexible
> for they shall not be
> bent out of shape.
>
> *Anonymous*

Whatever burdens my fellow caregivers struggle with, I can help. I'm willing to put it all out there. The question is, are you willing to learn from the insights, wisdom, experience, and even failures—gleaned from watching over someone with a broken body for three decades?

If you're gasping for air, you can't help other people.

Sandra Rankin

I have come to believe that caring for myself is not
an act of indulgence. It is an act of survival.

Audre Lorde

---

*But the Lord is faithful; he will strengthen you
and guard you from the evil one.*

2 Thessalonians 3:3 NLT

Chapter 2

THE DELTA DOCTRINE

> It don't take too much I.Q.
> To see what you're doin' to me
> You better think.
> *Aretha Franklin and Ted White*

One day, while flying to Atlanta on Delta Airlines, (**D**uh, **E**verything **L**eaves **T**hrough **A**tlanta), I discovered that flight attendants state the best advice for caregivers—all day long:

> "In the unlikely event of the loss of cabin pressure, oxygen masks will drop from the ceiling. Securely place your mask on first, before helping anyone next to you who may need assistance."

That small directive, which I call the "Delta Doctrine," contains applicable wisdom for so many circumstances—but probably none as poignant as for those of us serving as a caregiver for a chronically ill or disabled loved one.

Compassion and love often mistakenly lead us to hold our own breath while trying to help someone else breathe. But once we make that decision, it is only a matter of time before we find ourselves gasping for air. And, if we are unable to breathe, how can we help anyone else?

Many of America's 65 million caregivers desperately try to assist a vulnerable loved one while growing dangerously close to "blacking out" themselves. Grabbing the mask first is not a sign of selfishness but rather the whisper of wisdom. Unfortunately, that soft voice is hard to hear over the often-deafening cries of someone we love.

Those who "push the wheelchair" serve as the critical team player for a suffering patient. Sadly, too many caregivers don't know how to create a sustainable care-structure for themselves. Simply getting sleep and eating a proper diet is not enough. Caregivers must remain healthy: physically, financially, emotionally, professionally, and spiritually. But staying healthy is impossible if we don't reach for the mask first.

Help is available, but caregivers must be willing to accept that help while tuning out the fear (and sometimes the panic) that can consume us during highly stressful moments.

On a plane, one must simply reach for the mask that dangles. For caregivers, however, reaching for help is different. Most of the conflicts that caregivers experience involve relationship dynamics. If the patient is bleeding or injured, then it is a medical crisis and that involves a different set of skills and needs, generally referred to as triage.

Caregiving scenarios that strain the bonds of friends, family, and marriage could benefit from "emotional triage." Since the one who suffers will, by definition, probably not be providing leadership in those areas, it is up to caregivers to ensure their own safety and well-being. Just as paramedics train to care for an agitated (and sometimes even violent) patient, caregivers can learn to protect their own emotional safety and peace of mind.

When the "turbulence of caregiving" hits, I've found three simple things that help me make healthy and positive decisions in high-stress moments: Wait, Water, and Walk.

Wait: Take a moment before responding. Regardless if the culprit is dementia, drugs, or just your loved one behaving badly, all types of "emotional tug-of-wars" seem to be happening simultaneously while caregiving. If you pick up the rope and involve yourself in a tug-of-war, one of two things will happen: You will win and end up on your rear, or you will lose and end up on your face.

Don't pick up the rope! Simply wait before responding. Rarely do you have to apologize or make amends for something you didn't say. Breathe slowly (inhale four seconds; exhale eight seconds), until you feel yourself growing calmer. Stress and anger are toxic for good decisions.

Water: Drink some cool water. It will buy you time to think more clearly. Avoid sugary drinks or even coffee, and instead grab a bottle or glass of water. Your body needs water—your brain needs water. From high blood pressure to fatigue, water helps a myriad of issues. A tanked-up brain functions better. Drink to think!

Walk: Caregiving creates extreme stress, so when things are bouncing off the walls, take a few moments to put on some comfortable shoes and walk off some of that tension. By doing so, you are truly putting on the mask first, getting better oxygen to your body and brain, and bleeding off anxiety. Walking immediately helps facilitate calmness. Settling yourself down allows you to bring your "A-Game" to the caregiving scenario.

Wait, Water, Walk cost little or nothing but can instantly help a caregiver make better decisions, calm down, and feel more at peace. These are the initial steps of the Delta Doctrine. "Put your mask on first" is the most responsible and caring step in your efforts to help others. In doing so, the patient gets a healthier, confident, stronger, and more "self-controlled" caregiver who can provide leadership while offering love.

Face your deficiencies and acknowledge them;

but do not let them master you.

Let them teach you patience, sweetness, insight.

When we do the best we can,

we never know what miracle is wrought in our life,

or in the life of another.

Helen Keller

———◦◦◦———

Take rest.

A field that has rested gives a beautiful crop.

Ovid

Chapter 3

———— ❧ ————

A DIFFERENT
PERSPECTIVE

*Perspective is everything when you are
experiencing the challenges of life.*

Joni Eareckson Tada

Sometimes, it helps to get a different perspective on a situation, in order for roles to be better defined. Let's start with a few qualifying questions:

Did you create the condition your loved one endures?

Can you cure them?

Can you control what is happening to them?

If you answered "yes" to these questions, then maybe this book is not for you. If you can create, cure, or control these types of life issues, then you don't need to worry about being a caregiver.

On the other hand, if you answered "no" to those questions, you are well on your way to understanding your powerlessness and inability to alter or change the circumstances facing you as a caregiver, and that's a good thing.

Although my résumé as a caregiver is a long and impressive one, I must confess that, not only have I failed to "fix" the situation; I can't stop it from getting worse. In fact, I can't even slow it down.

Mulling over these facts, it dawns upon me that maybe I have a different role to play in this scenario.

If controlling it or curing it is impossible, then what is my job as a caregiver? After decades of putting on the cape and mask and acting like a superhero every time a medical crisis pops up (often daily), I'm learning that my role is to love my wife, do the best I can, and grow as a healthy individual to the best of my abilities.

As capable as I am, it is abundantly clear that I am powerless over her injuries and equally powerless to take away any of her considerable pain. I do, however, have an important role to play but can only serve in that role if I am thinking and living in a healthy manner.

When I first started on this journey, I put my life on hold to help her life improve. After doing this for some time, it dawned upon me that I could not wait for her to get better—or worse—before I took steps to live a healthy life.

"Oh yes, my friend, you would have fought very bravely, and died very quickly."

Don Diego to Alejandro, The Mask of Zorro

When in the hospital dealing with a medical crisis, the normal response is to stop everything and throw ourselves recklessly at the issue. When the problems drag on for months, years, and decades, a plan must be implemented to help the caregiver build a healthy life.

That night in the hospital so long ago, I wouldn't have been able to process a "how-to" manual that required even more of the precious resources I spent every day. I needed something simple, attainable, practical, and able to do "right now."

What does that look like?

It looks like implementing easy-to-accomplish consistent steps to address the six major "HELP ME" impact areas affected by caregiving:

Health

Emotions

Lifestyle

Profession

Money

Endurance

Focusing on the health of the caregiver is not selfish or self-centered; in fact, it is the opposite.

By not seeking a healthy life of my own (physically, fiscally, and mentally), I risk greater harm to the one I love. As her sole support system, her well-being is jeopardized if I make unhealthy choices. If your own life is a ticking time bomb waiting to cause massive damage to one you love, it kind of makes it hard to wear the label "caregiver," doesn't it?

My perspective required changing. Healthy caregivers make better caregivers.

—➤◆◀—

Go to bed.

Whatever you're staying up for isn't worth it.

—

Andy Rooney

—➤◆◀—

No life can surpass that of a man who
quietly continues to serve God in the place where
providence has placed him.

C. H. Spurgeon

Find out where you can render a service; then render it.
The rest is up to the Lord.

S. S. Kresge

Some people give time, some give money,
some their skills and connections,
some literally give their life's blood.
But everyone has something to give.

Barbara Bush

Chapter 4

YOUR DECISION
TO SERVE

"The greatest among you will be your servant."
Matthew 23:11 HCSB

So you've decided to be a caregiver. There, I said it. You've *decided* to be a caregiver. You're probably thinking, *Peter, you don't understand. I didn't decide to take this job; it was forced upon me.*

Well, if that's what you're thinking, I respectfully disagree. Since you're reading this book, I'm pretty sure you've decided not to run away (at least not quite yet!). And you still consider yourself to be a "giver of care." You've made the decision to participate, and stay, in the marathon called caregiving, and that indicates something special about you! Here's why:

According to the greatest, and most often-quoted source in human history, the carpenter from Nazareth, you are among a group He calls "the greatest of these." According to Jesus, you're not middle-of-the-pack, and you're not bringing up the rear. Because of your decision to serve, He maintains that you have reached the pinnacle of earthly success. And if He believes it, who are you to say otherwise?

Everybody can be great because anybody can serve.

Martin Luther King, Jr.

Are you feeling a little isolated, or fearful, or decidedly *un*successful? Well those feelings are totally understandable because you live in a world that glorifies power, prestige, fame, and money. In this world, awards go to CEOs, movie stars, professional athletes, and supermodels—rarely caregivers who volunteer to care for a suffering human being for months, years, and even decades.

But the words of Jesus teach us that the most esteemed men and women on this planet are not the widely recognized faces we see on magazine covers. The greatest among us are those who serve. And that includes you.

When the unrelenting demands of caregiving leave you gasping for air, you may not feel like a rip-roaring success. In fact, when the bills pile high and the paperwork piles higher, you may believe (quite wrongly) that genuine success is out of your reach.

When those feelings wash over you, I refer you to a Higher Authority who has already awarded you with life's greatest merit badge. Because you've decided to stay, to serve, and to care—you're esteemed by God Himself.

Hope deferred makes the heart sick.

Proverbs 13:12 NKJV

We hope vaguely but dread precisely.

Paul Valéry

You can't connect the dots looking forward; you can only connect them looking backwards. So you have to trust that the dots will somehow connect in your future.

Steve Jobs

And we rejoice in the hope of the glory of God.
Not only that, but we rejoice in our sufferings, knowing that suffering produces endurance, and endurance produces character, and character produces hope, and hope does not put us to shame, because God's love has been poured into our hearts through the Holy Spirit who has been given to us.

Romans 5:2–7 ESV

Chapter 5

HOPE FOR
THE CAREGIVER

They overcame by the blood of the Lamb
and the word of their testimony.

Revelation 12:11 NKJV (emphasis added)

Every day, I encounter caregivers who are struggling to keep their heads—and their hearts—above water. Oftentimes, these men and women have made heroic sacrifices for their loved ones, yet they still feel a vague sense of guilt. Sometimes, they feel afraid, or grief-stricken, or anxious. Or perhaps they feel nothing at all; they just feel numb.

While each journey is unique, the constant grind leads many to share the common feeling of hopelessness. Not only disheartening for the caregiver, that feeling also bleeds over to well-meaning people who try to console, but sadly miss the mark.

Over the years, others have tried to offer consolation to Gracie and me when they see the challenges we live with.

"I hate what you have to go through, but look at the testimony," is an often-repeated phrase. Another one is, "Your burdens are great, but look what God has done through you all through your Standing With Hope ministry." Further still, we've often heard the *consolation of speculation*. "God clearly has a plan and purpose for all this, or you wouldn't be here."

> My hope is built on nothing less
> Than Jesus' blood and righteousness.
>
> *Edward Mote*

I appreciate the sentiment behind those statements, but they are just that: sentiment, and sentiment is not hope. A great testimony and even a powerful ministry to Gracie's fellow amputees is not a consolation prize for the harshness of our lives. As wonderful as our work is, that is not what strengthens our hearts during brutal times. Our consolation has to be greater than simply doing good works and even having a great message.

The challenges of this world are crushing and will bust you up—and beat you down. We've all seen too many individuals experience harsh events, and then all too quickly promote a testimony of their journey, but then fall apart under the hot lights of fame and exposure. The "testimony" alone can't sustain, and does not offer long term hope.

It seems too many mix "testimony" with "inspirational message." According to Revelation 12:11, they ". . . overcame by the blood of the Lamb and the word of their testimony." Our testimony is bearing witness to the work and its Author. That's why telling those who struggle that they have a great testimony is missing the mark. Pointing to the Author, rather than the testimony offers tangible hope.

When your wife is seizing, going into respiratory arrest, screaming in agony, or listlessly looking off and living in a place where she can't be reached, no ministry or testimony provides consolation in those moments. What I hang my hat on is far greater than those things—and that's what helps me push back against the hopelessness.

Standing alone in hospital corridors, raging at my powerlessness, watching Gracie grimacing in pain, daily checking to see if she's breathing, or hanging my head in weariness, I depend upon a greater source of hope and consolation than what my mind, and the minds of others, can fully comprehend.

Trust in the LORD with all your heart and lean not unto your own understanding. In all your ways acknowledge Him, and He shall direct your paths.

Proverbs 3:5–6 NKJV

————◆————

Worry is interest paid on trouble before it comes due.

William Ralph Inge

————◆————

The very anxiety which arises through your difficulty leaves you unfit to meet that difficulty.

C. H. Spurgeon

————◆————

Let our advance worrying become advance thinking and planning.

Winston Churchill

Chapter 6

---❈❈❈---

DON'T BELIEVE
EVERYTHING
YOU THINK

Worry does not empty tomorrow of its sorrow.
It empties today of its strength.

Corrie ten Boom

Just because you're worried about it doesn't mean it's
actually going to happen. We have enough to consider for
today. Our fears tempt us to indulge in the pain of things that
may not even come to pass, and it's all too easy to live in the
wreckage of our future.

When learning that my wife contracted a terrible infection following back surgery, I grew even more dismayed to
hear that she would require three months on her back in the
hospital, with multiple operations to irrigate the infection

out of her spinal area. Listening to her surgeon, my heart sank and the fear rose. He'd known me for sixteen years at that point, and he looked at me with compassion while I stated with disbelief, "I can't do this for three months."

"We're not focusing on three months. We're focusing on today," he said while putting his hand on my shoulder.

"Tomorrow will take care of itself."

"Give us this day our daily bread" sounds great from the pulpit until you have to live it out every day. Our culture simply doesn't lend itself to living one day at a time, but as caregivers, we must.

My mind is a dangerous neighborhood to go to by myself.

Morry Ellis

Our minds will play tricks on us, and we indulge ourselves in horrific scenarios that get us worked up into a froth. How much control do we truly have over any of this?

Admittedly, most of what we fret about is "fret worthy," but it doesn't change the fact that we are powerless over a great deal of it. If we can't change it or cure it, then we certainly aren't going to do much good worrying over it. By training our minds, we can slowly walk our troubled hearts away from the cliff of worry and live in the moment—and be content with the "daily bread" we have.

My best thinking took me down into some dark places. I choose not to believe everything I think, and instead appeal to what God thinks about my circumstances—and, more importantly, what He thinks about His abilities. As a caregiver, I've learned that no one can do this for a lifetime—but anyone can do it for twenty-four hours.

So do not worry about tomorrow;
for tomorrow will care for itself.
Each day has enough trouble of its own.
Matthew 6:34 NASB

It is a dreadful truth that the state of having to depend
solely on God is what we all dread most.
It is good of Him to force us, but dear me,
how hard to feel that it is good at the time.

C. S. Lewis

———◦◦◦———

Thank you Lord Jesus for the privilege of serving you in
your many horrible disguises.

Mother Teresa

———◦◦◦———

In thee, O LORD, do I put my trust.
Psalm 31:1 KJV

Chapter 7

OBLIGATION
IS A PETRI DISH FOR
RESENTMENT

Nothing becomes an obligation simply
because someone tells you it is.

David Seabury

Obligation is a horrible taskmaster and a poor motivator for caregiving. Feeling required to do and care for another often leads to bitterness and resentment. After a while, nothing our loved one does "is right," and the building resentment can erupt into painful outbursts that only add more misery to an already miserable situation.

You may be trying to do too much, bearing too much weight on your own shoulders, trying to do everything by yourself. When our hearts carry that kind of burden, it's like trying to push a wheelchair with clenched fists, or angrily screaming "I Love You!" It doesn't work.

Being responsible doesn't mean obligated. Responsibility reflects duty. Obligation stems from being coerced or forced. Responsibility fosters stewardship. Obligation breeds resentment.

We can only do our best, and the rest has to belong to the rightful owner: God. Our loved ones have a Savior, and we are not that savior.

We push back against obligation by reminding ourselves that we are stewards not owners and by cultivating a servant's heart. The loved one receiving our care, however, is not our master. That belongs only to God.

———◆———

"It is not enough to do, one must also become.
I wish to be wiser, stronger, better. This—"
I held out my hands "—this thing that is me
is incomplete. It is only the raw material with
which I have to work. I want to make it
better than I received it."

—

Louis L'Amour, Jubal Sackett

———◆———

The ideal man bears the accidents of life with dignity and grace, making the best of circumstances.

Aristotle

———◆———

I am careful not to confuse excellence with perfection. Excellence I can reach for; perfection is God's business.

Michael J. Fox

Chapter 8

---⊰❈⊱---

PROGRESS
NOT PERFECTION

*Do not lose courage in considering
your own imperfections.*

St. Francis of Sales

As caregivers, we'd like to be perfect. We'd like to do everything for our loved ones while taking the perfect amount of time for ourselves. We'd like to have enough energy to accomplish everything on our to-do lists, and when the day is done, we'd like to get a "perfect" eight hours of sleep.

Reality, however, daily reminds us that those things are rarely possible. We can't be the "perfect" caregivers—nobody can. And that's okay. God doesn't expect us to lead a mistake-free lives, and neither should we.

We will make mistakes, but those are teachable moments that can move us further into wisdom. As we go through the daily grind of caregiving, and as we endure the real-world challenges that are woven into the fabric of our daily responsibilities, we can be forgiving of our own shortcomings.

When it comes to being a healthy caregiver, seek progress not perfection. Simply do your best, day by day and moment by moment. God is perfect enough for all of us, and if you or I were perfect, we wouldn't need a Savior, would we?

When mistakes are made, offer forgiveness to others—starting with the person you see in the mirror. And then, leave the rest up to God. Forgiveness doesn't mean it wasn't important. Forgiveness means taking our hands off someone else's throat—even if it's our own throat. Since healing usually takes longer than forgiveness, it's helpful and wise to give ourselves (and others) time to heal.

Keep boundaries, lose the grudges.

We are only stewards and have little or no power to change the circumstances our loved ones carry. Smacking ourselves or others around for making a mistake will offer no help to the one we love.

If the mistake was mine, I'm learning to own it, make amends, and grow through the process.

———◆———

To progress is always to begin
always to begin again.

—

Martin Luther, Commentary on Romans

———◆———

What cannot be altered must be borne, not blamed.

Thomas Fuller

———◆———

Accept the place the divine providence
has found for you.

Ralph Waldo Emerson

———◆———

We must make the best of those ills
that cannot be avoided.

Alexander Hamilton

———◆———

I pray hard, work hard, and leave the rest to God.

Florence Griffith Joyner

Chapter 9

WHAT TO DO ABOUT THE THINGS THAT CAN'T BE CHANGED

Accept things as they are, not as you wish them to be.

Napoleon Bonaparte

Understanding and accepting that a caregiver is powerless to make someone else happy or miserable is important to maintaining a healthy independence from the person receiving care. Their state may be awful, even pitiful, but it is still their state and their joy, or lack thereof. We can be polite, caring, attentive, and upbeat, but they have to choose their own emotional and mental state.

I've seen individuals in severe pain who exuded joy and happiness, but I've also met people with minimal pain who exude misery.

If your loved one is miserable, must you be? If your loved one is an amputee, must you be? If your loved one is in a wheelchair, must you be? Their pain is just that: *their pain*. We can hate it for them. It can break our hearts. At the end of the day, however, we remain powerless to lift this burden from them.

We can and must function as independent individuals, regardless of how intertwined our lives are on the "journey of suffering patient and caregiver." It's not easy, but it is possible.

> We must accept life as it goes along and do the best with the hand we've been dealt.
>
> *Bobby Allison*

The key is detaching but with love. Sometimes the weariness and frustration tempt us to detach with extreme prejudice. That's not detaching; that's severing. An amputation isn't required in order to detach; rather it's a simple unlocking. The key to unlocking is knowing the limits and boundaries.

Life has a way of unfolding, not as we will, but as it will. And sometimes, there is precious little we can do to change things. When events transpire that are beyond our control, we have a choice: learn the art of acceptance, or make ourselves miserable as we struggle to change the unchangeable. We cannot cure, change, or control the terrible things our loved ones endure. The only thing we can control is our own thoughts, our words, and our deeds.

You could write a song about some kind of
emotional problem you are having, but it would not be
a good song, in my eyes, until it went through
a period of sensitivity to a moment of clarity.
Without that moment of clarity to contribute
to the song, it's just complaining.

Joni Mitchell

———◆———

*"Then you will know the truth,
and the truth will set you free."*

John 8:32 NIV

Chapter 10

---⊰⊱---

REALISTIC
EXPECTATIONS

*Real life is, to most of us, a perpetual compromise
between the ideal and the possible.*

Bertrand Russell

For many caregivers, facing reality is difficult. After all,
we want our loved ones to find healing. As we wish
and-wait for their recovery, we're tempted to set unrealistic
expectations for ourselves and for our loved ones. When we
do, we're setting everybody up for biggie-sized portions of
frustration and disappointment.

It's taken me many years to discover and admit that I am
powerless over Gracie's challenges. Despite my love for her,
and despite my best efforts, I cannot take away her chronic
pain. I desperately wish that I could, but I can't.

As a double-amputee with prosthetic limbs, Gracie falls on occasion. I can't prevent it, and it breaks my heart when it happens.

But it's reality. And in my better moments, I accept our world as it is, not as I wish it would be. I've come to appreciate realistic expectations. Reality can be a tough companion at times, but it's an honest friend.

Facing reality doesn't mean abandoning hope. And it doesn't mean giving up.

Facing reality means accepting the world as it is. As we do so, it's important to remember that as we face the caregiver's reality, we can accept that world while also working to make it a little better for at least two people: ourselves and our loved ones.

———»•«———

Life is not a problem to be solved,
but a reality to be experienced.

—

Søren Kierkegaard

———»•«———

Finally brothers, whatever is true,
whatever is honorable,
whatever is just, whatever is pure,
whatever is lovely, whatever is commendable—
if there is any moral excellence and if there is any praise—
dwell on these things.

Philippians 4:8 HCSB

———⊰•⊱———

If you carry joy in your heart,
you can heal any moment.

Carlos Santana

———⊰•⊱———

The trouble with many men is that they have
got just enough religion to make them miserable.
If there is not joy in religion,
you have got a leak in your religion.

Billy Sunday

Chapter 11

WE'RE AS MISERABLE OR
AS HAPPY AS WE MAKE
OURSELVES

Nehemiah said, "Go and enjoy choice food and sweet drinks,
and send some to those who have nothing prepared.
This day is sacred to our Lord. Do not grieve,
for the joy of the LORD is your strength."

Nehemiah 8:10 NIV

I've seen joyful caregivers, and I've seen miserable ones. For the joyful ones, I think, that the ones who abandoned their desire to be CEO of the universe tend to exercise their newfound freedom with joy. It's a terrible thing to feel as if you have to be in charge of everything.

Here's a simple test: Look down at your hands. Do you see nail prints?

No? Well, good news: you're not in charge. That realization means that you don't have to carry things that aren't yours.

They're going to bleed.
They're going to fall.
They're going to suffer.
They're going to die.

You cannot stop those things from happening. Spending your life trying to stave off the inevitable is the fastest route to bitterness, resentment, hopelessness, and even insanity.

Spending your days doing what you have control over (your thoughts, words, and deeds) and leaving the rest to God is the only way to peace, calmness, and yes, joy.

Joy is not the absence of challenges and pain: that's numbness. Gracie can be out of pain today, but she would be numb from anesthesia drugs. Would her joy increase?

I once quoted Gracie in a song I wrote,

"Sometimes the pain each day can bring
clouds the joy that is there."

"The Love of Jesus," Peter W. Rosenberger and Hank Martin

There is joy; there is happiness. Pain and heartache can only cloud it, not remove it. Will we choose to trust that joy is there when it's not seen or felt?

As caregivers, we daily look at grim and harsh things—but must we be grim and harsh ourselves?

I've learned that even when all of your senses are screaming at you, joy is still there. If we allow it to, joy can even hold us as we grieve.

Hope for the Caregiver is the conviction that we can live calmer, healthier, and even more joyful lives—even while staring at brutal circumstances.

The moment we choose to slip our scared hands into his scarred hands, we embrace something that transcends the pain we currently face. Even in the sorrow each day brings, there waits a joy beyond our understanding.

PART II

———— ❦ ————

EMOTIONS

The cheerful heart has a continual feast.

Proverbs 15:15 NIV

I take my emotions and funnel them
into something positive.

Brian Wilson

The spiritual life is a life beyond moods.
It is a life in which we choose joy and do not allow
ourselves to become victims of passing feelings
of happiness or depression.

Henri Nouwen

———◦———

"Well done, good and faithful servant; you were faithful
over a few things, I will make you ruler over many things.
Enter into the joy of your lord."

Matthew 25:21 NKJV

Chapter 12

NAVIGATING THROUGH
THE EMOTIONAL FOG

*There are good and there are bad times, but our mood
changes more often than our fortune.*

Jules Renard

Caregivers bounce all over the emotional map between
compassion and frustration, between obligation and
commitment. The lines get so blurry at times, that caregivers
often find themselves operating out of intense Fear, Obligation, and Guilt (FOG) . . . which leads to Heartache, Anger,
and Turmoil (HAT).

Get it? In a FOG with a HAT? FOG HAT! (I like
'70's music.)

How do ships and planes navigate through a FOG?
They use a GPS (Global Positioning System), of course. So,
why not people?

FEAR

OBLIGATION

GUILT

Can be navigated by using a **GPS**

GRACE

PURPOSE

STEWARDSHIP

Human emotions are highly variable, decidedly unpredictable, and often unreliable. Our emotions are like the weather, only far more fickle. So we must learn to live by faith, not by the ups and downs of our own emotional roller coasters.

Who is in charge of your emotions? Is it you? Or have you formed the unfortunate habit of letting other people—or troubling situations—determine the quality of your thoughts and the direction of your day? Do you wake up every day and ask someone else what kind of day you will have?

As a caregiver with big responsibilities, you owe it to yourself *and* your loved one to learn how to control your emotions before your emotions control you.

Sometime soon, you will probably be gripped by negative emotions (think FOG HAT), and at first, you'll believe everything you think. Take the time to catch yourself before those emotions run wild. To navigate through your emotional fog, use God's GPS (Grace, Purpose, and Stewardship). And while you're at it, turn the ultimate outcome over to God.

Your emotions will incvitably change; God will not. I recall a farmer in Ghana named Kwame who received a prosthetic limb from our organization, Standing With Hope. The entire time we made the limb, he complained about his amputation. After receiving his prosthesis from us, I sat down with him and offered, "Kwame, I know you are bitter about the loss of your leg. I know that you blame God for allowing the amputation." Motioning to Gracie across the room, I also pointed to the high performance prosthetic foot on Kwame's new prosthesis. "Kwame, that foot belonged to my wife. She gave one of her prosthetic feet so that you could walk. She trusted God with the loss of both of her legs, and now you are literally able to stand . . . on her faith." As he looked at me with widening eyes, I added, "Each step you take, I want you to remember you are doing so on her faith."

Kwame started a life of trusting God, one footstep at a time. Within a short time, he was walking, and even running.

How is our journey any different? Today is a good day to take one step of faith . . . and trust that God is working in your life and circumstances in ways that you can't possibly imagine.

More Thoughts about Your Personal GPS and about Grace

My grace is sufficient for you, for My strength
is made perfect in weakness.

2 Corinthians 12:9 NKJV

⸻

The grace of God is sufficient for all our needs, for every
problem, and for every difficulty, for every broken heart,
and for every human sorrow.

Peter Marshall

⸻

God's grace is just the right amount of just the right quality
arriving as if from nowhere at just the right time.

Bill Bright

⸻

Let us therefore come boldly to the throne of grace, that we may
obtain mercy and find grace to help in time of need.

Hebrews 4:16 NKJV

About Purpose

First say to yourself what you would be;
then do what you have to do.

Epictetus

———◆———

You're the only one who can do what you do.

Lois Evans

———◆———

Do something worth remembering.

Elvis Presley

———◆———

For it is God who is working in you,
enabling you both to desire and to work out His good purpose.

Philippians 2:13 HCSB

About Stewardship

As each one has received a gift, minister it to one another,
as good stewards of the manifold grace of God.

1 Peter 4:10 NKJV

———◆———

Employ whatever God has entrusted you with,
in doing good, all possible good,
in every possible kind and degree.

John Wesley

———◆———

God doesn't want your ability—he wants your availability.

Bobby Bowden

———◆———

When he was young, I told Dale Jr. that hunting and
racing are a lot alike. Holding that steering wheel and
holding that rifle both mean you better be responsible.

Dale Earnhardt

You must look in to other people—as well as at them.

Lord Chesterfield

———◆———

Love is a great beautifier.

Louisa May Alcott

———◆———

Love is patient, love is kind and is not jealous;
love does not brag and is not arrogant, does not act
unbecomingly; it does not seek its own, is not provoked,
does not take into account a wrong suffered, does not rejoice
in unrighteousness, but rejoices with the truth; bears all things,
believes all things, hopes all things, endures all things.

1 Corinthians 13:4–7 NASB

Chapter 13

SEE THE HEART,
NOT THE CHART

I pray that your love for each other will overflow more
and more, and that you will keep on growing
in your knowledge and understanding.

Philippians 1:9 NLT

Sometimes, caregiving seems to be an all-consuming task. The magnitude of the job places such a strain on the relationship that the tender flower of love is often crushed under the massive weight of daily medical crises. Although triage, medical procedures, and medically related tasks are important, they are *not* the relationship. The cry of the heart is often drowned by the moan of the body, and it takes time and practice to differentiate between the two.

When you find that the entire conversation revolves around medical information, that's a clear indicator that the matters of the heart are being shoved aside. Use that moment to look beyond the tubes, beyond the casts, the wheelchairs, the colostomies, the prosthetic limbs, the pills, and all the other distractions. Ignore the treatments and look, instead, at the person.

When Jesus healed the paralyzed man lowered through the roof, He first addressed the condition of his heart by forgiving his sins. He saw past the medical circumstances and spoke to the greater need of the heart.

We can model that, if we choose. It's rarely easy, and it will cost us our dignity, pride, and ego. Loving someone has that effect. The one we care for may not recognize or even appreciate what we do on their behalf, and that's okay—if we love them, we're doing it for their benefit not ours. Being angry while trying to care for them isn't helpful or sustainable; it's about keeping our hearts tender—while seeing their heart.

Keeping our hearts tender is not easy. Caregiving contains many flashpoints, and it's all too easy to pop off and say and do hurtful things. We often find ourselves at the breaking point, and that makes it exponentially harder to focus on the relationship with our loved one, when our emotions are already fried.

A caller to my radio show once asked, "How can I communicate to my loved one that I can't handle it anymore—that it's coming off the rails?"

My reply was, "The person who needs to hear it's coming off the rails is not your loved one . . . it's you—and preferably in the presence of a counselor."

We can't take for granted that the one we care for can understand our frustration. My brother has a twenty-six-year-old daughter born with cerebral palsy and severe cognitive impairments. Taking care of her is like caring for a giant baby. Kelsey cannot process what my brother and sister-in-law go through. She just lives her life.

Developmental issues, narcotics, alcohol, or a variety of other impairments may prevent an empathy towards your circumstances. Chronic pain and disease have a way of blocking the field of view for folks, and all they can see is their own need. Some days, quite bluntly, they're just having a bad day and, even if they could, they won't process your feelings.

Reacting to their behavior will only heap more frustration, rage, and ultimately guilt upon you. Don't put yourself in a position to fight with them, and regardless of how they behave, we never get a "free pass to be an ass." It's okay to detach from those feelings and their behavior. As you learn to serve for a higher reason than just the immediate, you will find that you can respond without reacting.

If they are abusive, then professionals (physicians, counselors, and even law enforcement) may need to be contacted. If, however, they are behaving poorly, try to remember that they are not doing it to you; they're just doing it. Some level of impairment or personality issue is driving their behavior.

You can still see past all of that and minister to the heart, and you don't have to go to every fight that you get a ticket to—you can sit a few of them out.

When cleaning up a mess or dressing a wound, I'd rather weep than grind my teeth.

I find it helps me when I think about how Christ willingly endured the cross on my behalf.

—

Christian love, either towards God or towards man, is an affair of the will.

—

C. S. Lewis

For I have learned in whatever situation I am to be content.
I know how to be brought low, and I know how to abound.
In any and every circumstance, I have learned the secret
of facing plenty and hunger, abundance and need. I can do
all things through him who strengthens me.

Philippians 4:11–13 ESV

——— ·◈· ———

The world ain't all sunshine and rainbows.
It's a very mean and nasty place and I don't care
how tough you are, it will beat you to your knees and
keep you there permanently if you let it. You, me,
or nobody is gonna hit as hard as life. But it ain't about
how hard you hit. It's about how hard you can get hit
and keep moving forward. How much you can take
and keep moving forward. That's how winning is done!

Sylvester Stallone as Rocky Balboa

Chapter 14

THE HARDEST JOB

Indeed we count them blessed who endure.

James 5:11 NKJV

Serving as a caregiver remains the hardest task I've ever accepted. With so many conflicting emotions, finding peace sometimes seems impossible. Torn between a deep love for my spouse and the thorny feelings associated with constant caring for the needs of another human being, I often close my eyes and think of a happy place. But sometimes, I still see myself decades ago at that hospital, hunched over Gracie's chart, covered with vomit, and my eyes filling with tears.

Mistakes? Oh, I've had ample time to make just about every kind of mistake one can. I've forgotten more mistakes than most caregivers will ever make. Yet, even those missteps can serve as valuable lessons to help shape how I deal with the stresses and challenges of caregiving.

I suppose that crying, "Help me!" is the first step in improving your life as a caregiver. But if you're one of those self-reliant, do-it-yourself, rugged individuals who doesn't like to ask for help, you may find it difficult to ask for the assistance you need, even when you're feeling overwhelmed.

Caregiving may be the hardest job you'll ever tackle. Don't try to tackle it alone. And don't try to tackle it by denying yourself the care you need to do the job right.

In almost thirty years of caregiving, I've learned many lessons. And I'm still learning. Most of all, I'm learning that although there are many things beyond my ability to change, I, however, can change. If nothing else, I am making progress at being content in the middle of very unsettling things. While far away from perfection, I am encouraged by the changes and personal growth I often glimpse.

—◆—

They're not doing it to you,
they're just doing it.

—

Anonymous

—◆—

Let's take Jesus at his word.

When he says we're forgiven, let's unload the guilt.

When he says we're valuable, let's believe him.

When he says we're eternal, let's bury our fear.

When he says we're provided for, let's stop worrying.

Max Lucado

———◆———

But they whose guilt within their bosoms lie

Imagine every eye beholds their blame.

Shakespeare

———◆———

Guilt is the gift that keeps on giving.

Erma Bombeck

———◆———

For the LORD your God is a merciful God. . . .

Deuteronomy 4:31 NIV

Chapter 15

BEYOND GUILT

Calvin: "There's no problem so awful, that you can't add some guilt to it and make it even worse."

Bill Watterson,

The Complete Calvin and Hobbes

Guilt comes from many sources, not just the big-time sins that get great press. So it's not surprising that caregivers, who make heroic sacrifices every day, still struggle mightily with guilt.

Being able to get up and walk while our loved one can't; jumping into the car to run errands while he or she is stuck at home; standing up in the shower while the other person must use the shower bench; being pain-free, while the loved one never knows a day without suffering. These are just a few examples of the guilt-inducing situations that may plague caregivers. And parents of disabled children may wrestle with intense guilt over the condition of sons or daughters born with physical or mental limitations they didn't ask for and can't fully understand.

In addition, we caregivers make mistakes, some of them grievous. We are, after all, fallible—and often exhausted—human beings. We trip over the same sins and vices that others do, but the immense pressure of caregiving often compresses our learning curve.

Most individuals experience a "slow growth" into maturity and life crises. But, as caregivers, we often find ourselves in life's "express lane," managing crisis after crisis, sometimes dealing with life-and-death issues. The stress from the nonstop barrage dulls our senses, and may even eat away at our moral compass. When we do fail, guilt from the failure gnaws at the soul. So we work even harder, denying ourselves more, thus adding more pressures to our already-stress-filled lives.

But guilt is not the answer. Guilt doesn't strengthen relationships; it destroys them. Caregivers can't effectively live and serve others while bearing so heavy a burden of shame or guilt.

So, we must apply grace to those guilty feelings. By consistently reminding ourselves that God's grace covers our sins, we discover that guilt no longer whips us into a frenzy. Grace frees us to love and to serve with a clean heart. Sometimes, remembering God's grace is not a day-to-day thing; it's a minute-to-minute lifeline.

My sin, oh, the bliss of this glorious thought!
My sin, not in part but the whole,
Is nailed to the cross, and I bear it no more,
Praise the Lord, praise the Lord, O my soul!

"It Is Well with My Soul"

Horatio Spafford

"In time, we hate that which we often fear."

William Shakespeare, Antony and Cleopatra

———◆◆———

*"Be strong and courageous, and do the work.
Do not be afraid or discouraged,
for the LORD God, my God, is with you."*

1 Chronicles 28:20 NIV

Chapter 16

FEAR IS A FOUR-LETTER WORD

No one ever told me that grief felt so like fear.

C. S. Lewis, A Grief Observed

Caregiving is not for the faint of heart. The demands are great; the stakes are high; the dangers are real, and, sometimes, so is the fear.

As a caregiver, you live in a world that can be a frightening place—and often, a discouraging place. You live in a world where life-changing losses can be painful and profound. But, with God's help, you can meet those challenges with confidence and calmness.

Many of the things we worry about never come to pass, yet we worry still. Worrying is indulging ourselves in the pain of things that may never happen. We worry about the future and the past; we worry about money, doctors, and insurance. As we survey the landscape of our lives, we observe all manner of molehills and we imagine them to be mountains. Sometimes, the mountains we see are real, but often they're not.

Are you concerned about the inevitable challenges of caregiving? If so, why not ask God to help you regain a clear perspective about the obstacles (and opportunities) that confront you? When you ask Him for help, He can touch your heart, clear your vision, renew your mind, and calm your fears.

During the darker days of life, we are wise to remember the words of Jesus, who reassured His disciples saying, "Take courage! It is I. Don't be afraid" (Matt. 14:27 NIV).

Peppered throughout the Bible, God continually reminds individuals and groups to "not be afraid." He knows that as we face things in life, we are scared spitless. He doesn't mock our fear; He calms it with His presence. Then, with God's comfort and His love in our hearts, we can offer encouragement to others. And by helping them face *their* fears, we can, in turn, tackle our own challenges with courage, determination, and faith. Feeling out of control scares us. Learning we don't have to be, relieves us.

The LORD is the One who will go before you. He will be with you; He will not leave you or forsake you. Do not be afraid or discouraged.

—

Deuteronomy 31:8 HCSB

All the lonely people, where do they all come from?

All the lonely people, where do they all belong?

"Eleanor Rigby," Paul McCartney/John Lennon

———⋅◈⋅———

Abide with me; fast falls the eventide;

The darkness deepens; Lord, with me abide;

When other helpers fail and comforts flee,

Help of the helpless, oh, abide with me.

"Abide with Me," Henry Francis Lyte

———⋅◈⋅———

Do not be inaccessible. None is so perfect that

he does not need at times the advice of others.

Baltasar Gracián

———⋅◈⋅———

We cannot live only for ourselves.

A thousand fibers connect us with our fellow men.

Herman Melville

Chapter 17

ISOLATION

Loneliness is the first thing which
God's eye named not good.

John Milton

At the onset of the condition, friends, family members, and others usually surround the situation with love, meals, kindness, and attention. As time progresses, relationships wax and wane—and new faces appear on the scene. But when the months drag into years (and even decades), relationships often fade, and a feeling of isolation may envelope the caregiver. Other people may simply not know the needs, or perhaps they can't find the words, or the situation just seems too uncomfortable to get involved.

Regardless of the reasons, time has a way of filtering relationships, and the caregiver is left to fend alone without meaningful interaction outside of a bleak situation that, at best, stays the same for long stretches. At worst, the situation deteriorates. If the condition worsens, more individuals may appear on the scene to provide additional help, but the increased level of support may also mean that a new plateau of loss is imminent.

Isolation often occurs due to logistics. Sometimes, it is not possible or practical for the caregiver to transport the loved one outside the home. Other times, caregivers, embarrassed about the condition of their loved ones—or wishing to protect their dignity—remove themselves from the public eye.

Yea, though I walk through the valley of the shadow of death, I will fear no evil; for Thou art with me.

Psalm 23:4 KJV

There are many reasons for the isolation that caregivers feel, but the results are universally negative. Without positive human connections, everybody suffers. That's why it's important for caregivers to remain engaged in church, community, and other social networks. And, since caregivers can often feel lonely in a crowded room, it's important not only to attend but also to engage.

If you're one of those caregivers who's experienced a gradual separation from the outside world, today's the day to reengage. Make the effort to jumpstart old friendships and discover new ones. Cultivate healthy relationships and find appropriate ways to reconnect with the world. It's critical to push back against the isolation. You may feel awkward at first, so take it slowly. Try to avoid grasping the connectivity out of desperation; instead, enjoy the moment. After wandering in the desert and being parched, it is unwise to guzzle water. Rather, it should be sipped slowly to rehydrate properly. We don't need to pin all our hopes for friendship on one phone call or a single lunch. There will be more.

You have to be what you are.
Whatever you are, that's what you gotta be.

Johnny Cash

———◦———

I'm Chevy Chase, and you're not.

Chevy Chase

———◦———

There are three things extremely hard:
steel, a diamond, and to know one's self.

Benjamin Franklin

Chapter 18

LOSS OF IDENTITY

This above all: to thine own self be true.

William Shakespeare

Hamlet Act 1: scene 3

A caregiver's identity can become lost in the world, and in the details, of the one they care for. Eventually, the caregiver begins to speak almost exclusively in the first-person plural ("we") or in the third-person singular ("he" or "she"). In such cases, a conscious effort is required for the caregiver to speak in first person ("I"). Although understandable, this loss of identity leads to many problems, including codependency, resentment, depression, and the inability to make independent (and critical) decisions.

Since other folks usually focus on the person in the wheelchair, the hurting caregiver may feel ignored. And on those infrequent occasions when someone *does* inquire about the caregiver's emotional state, the caregiver may have a difficult time answering the question.

The flip-side of identity-loss is "over-sharing." Some caregivers have been so deprived of attention and interaction that their neediness gets the better of them. So, they make people "drink from the fire hose" by dousing listeners with way too much information. Given that a truckload of emotions may tumble out to the first sincere person who asks, it's usually a good idea to breathe slowly while thinking about each word.

If you're a caregiver who finds it hard to speak in the first person, it's time to reclaim your identity. Using the "I-word" may feel awkward at first, even stress-inducing. But please don't give up. Sharing from the heart takes practice and trust, but you're worth it.

I promise.

When a codependent dies,
someone else's life flashes in front of their eyes.

—

Unknown

PART III

<hr/>

LIFESTYLE

Thou wilt show me the path of life . . . .

Psalm 16:11 KJV

Life is like a game of cards.
The hand that is dealt you represents determinism;
the way you play it is free will.

Jawaharlal Nehru

Now that my life is so prearranged
I know that it's time for a cool change.

The Little River Band, Glenn Shorrock

———◆———

Happy is he who makes daily progress and
who considers not what he did yesterday
but what advance he can make today.

St. Jerome

———◆———

Greater love has no one than this,
than to lay down one's life for his friends.

John 15:13 NKJV

Chapter 19

SUSTAINABILITY

You may have to fight a battle
more than once to win it.

Margaret Thatcher

I'm frequently asked by non-caregivers "How do I help them . . . they seem so capable." It's often hard to know what it looks like to help a high-functioning "multi-tasker" who seems capable of managing chaos, but don't be intimidated by their skill sets. Those abilities come from years of practice and repetitive behavior.

When I sit down at the piano, it looks like my fingers have a life of their own, but in reality listeners hear the culmination of decades of practice and instruction. Caregivers repeat many of the same tasks over and over, while simultaneously learning from a teacher far more demanding than even the strictest of my piano professors—fear.

Fear drives the desire we caregivers feel to wield control in an uncontrollable situation. When the wheels seem to be coming off, many of us panic and attempt to be superhuman. When presiding over a loved one's decline and suffering, it won't be tidy, and it may not get better. Yet how many of us recklessly hurl ourselves at a set of circumstances without regards to insuring sustainability?

> It's not that
> I'm so smart;
> it's just that I stay
> with problems longer.
>
> *Albert Einstein*

Simply because our loved one is sick or disabled doesn't guarantee we will outlive them. Yet how many caregivers structure their lives in that manner? Think of all the caregivers not seeing their own doctor regularly (72% are reported as failing to maintain regular visits with their personal physician). Think of all the caregivers who don't have life insurance. Think of all the caregivers who jeopardize their jobs by not having adequate communication with supervisors and a healthy professional plan. The list goes on of caregivers who fail to "put their mask on first."

Decades ago, I learned how to be a patient advocate with doctors, hospitals, and insurance companies—a skill that is not as complicated as one might think. Advocacy, however, is only one component of serving as a caregiver. When the crisis *du jour* of caring for a vulnerable loved one hits, I daily remind myself (and ask others to remind me) to "put my mask on first." Fear and panic never seem to take a holiday, so the battle is not in negotiating with America's health care system; it's in navigating the complex landmines of fear that lie in the heart.

The vast caregiving community is filled with people from all walks of life. Because you're reading this book, you're probably a member of that community, perhaps a longstanding member. If so, you already know the demands of the job you've taken on. You know the rewards and the pain; you know the exhilaration and the exhaustion, the isolation and the loneliness.

Throughout this book, I'll encourage you to practice *sustainable* caregiving. I'll ask you to think long and hard about the Delta Doctrine. And I'll try my best to persuade you that, if I can do it, so can you.

With the help of others who walk this journey, you and I can face that fear and make those tough unilateral decisions with the confidence that we care for our loved ones best—when we are doing so from a healthy, calm, and sustainable place.

Ask not what you can do for your country.
Ask what's for lunch.

Orson Welles

———◦◦◦———

Attention to one's life-style, especially in the direction
of reducing emotional tensions, a modest but
regular program of daily exercise, a diet low in salt
and sugar and reasonably free of fatty meats and fried foods,
and plenty of good drinking water—
all these are useful and indeed essential.

Norman Cousins

———◦◦◦———

Eat to live, and not live to eat.

Ben Franklin

Chapter 20

DIET

"I got so big, I had to put on my belt with a boomerang."

"I got so big, I got a shoe shine,
and had to take the man's word for it."

"I got so big, my nickname became: DAANNNNGG!"

It's certainly acceptable to stop for fast food or grab something on the fly when a loved one is at the hospital or having a crisis. Caregivers, however, often deal with lengthy hospital stays and daily crises. Eventually, fast food becomes a problem, and our bodies cry out for healthy sustenance. As caregivers, we know what's good and not good to eat, so there's no need to offer a diet plan, particularly when our world is full of those. Let's instead look at this topic philosophically.

As caregivers, we feel unsettled when we don't feel in control. That unsettledness screams for comfort, and food is just a refrigerator away. To make matters worse, we're tired. And cooking is work. Weariness and stress are quickly abated by high-fat, high-calorie food. Raw broccoli just can't compare to a pastrami on rye.

Given that we are playing for inches and not miles, we shouldn't feel the need to lease out the backyard to the farmer's market and go overboard. We should, instead, take small, manageable steps toward a more healthy diet.

Grab a bottle of water, not soda. At the grocery store, pick up a bag of apples instead of those fat-laden snacks. Even a few small choices in purchasing and preparing food can result in positive results.

Make a small choice today to eat something healthy instead of something comforting. Tomorrow, do it again, and make one additional healthy choice. Before you know it, you will have trained your body, and in doing so you will have improved your emotions, your lifestyle, and your overall state of mind.

—⟶◆⟵—

All you need is love.
But a little chocolate now and then doesn't hurt.

—

Charles M. Schulz

—⟶◆⟵—

The best heath care combines self-care
with professional advice.

Tom Ferguson, M.D.

———◆———

I told my psychiatrist that everyone hates me.
He said I was being ridiculous—everyone hasn't met me yet.

Rodney Dangerfield

———◆———

"Ask, and God will give to you.
Search, and you will find.
Knock, and the door will open for you.
Yes, everyone who asks will receive.
Everyone who searches will find.
And everyone who knocks will have the door opened."

Matthew 7:7–8 NCV

Chapter 21

COUNSELING HELPS

Where there is no guidance, a people falls,
but in an abundance of counselors there is safety.

Proverbs 11:14 LSV

To help them sort through some of the craziness, caregivers need a trained professional, whether a psychiatrist, psychologist, social worker, or other certified mental health counselor.

Referrals can come from a variety of sources, including family physicians and pastors, and many workplaces have an Employee Assistance Program (EAP). Visits through the EAP are often limited to a half-dozen. After that, a transition plan coalesces, and further counseling becomes the employee's responsibility. I've taken advantage of those services and heartily recommend it to others. Insurance may or may not pay for visits to counselors. One visit a month, however, is well worth the cost. (Keep your receipts for tax purposes.)

Since caregivers rarely deal with short-term issues, long-term counseling is strongly advisable. Licensed clinical social workers and licensed mental health counselors (I like to call them the "work horses of the counseling industry") offer a tremendous source of help at affordable fees.

Counseling is an area where churches often excel. Pastors can be a great resource for caregivers, but in most cases, pastors are not able to provide continuing care. Most clergy members are well acquainted with qualified counselors and can probably refer to and transition the long-term counseling needs.

> I always say shopping is cheaper than a psychiatrist.
>
> *Tammy Fay Bakker*

Sometimes, a church benevolence committee will underwrite a counselor's fees, especially if church members know that their contribution will provide tangible and immediate help to someone who is dealing with an intractable situation. But even if the church can't provide long-term counseling services, the best strategy for most caregivers is straightforward: find a trained mental health professional and figure out the most practical way to engage the counselor on a regular basis. It's a sensible way to ensure that you're caring for yourself first, so that you can best care for your loved one.

If you attend a religious group that advises against counseling, you might want to rethink your participation with such a group. Pastors and other religious leaders who preach against counseling probably haven't walked through enough heartache of this kind and speak out of ignorance, so give them a wide berth.

A guy goes to the psychiatrist and says,
"Doc, I'm having the same dream every night that I'm either
a tee-pee or a wig-wam . . . what does it mean?!"
"Oh, that's easy," replied the psychiatrist.
"It just means you are too tents!"

A really old joke told to me by my father.

———— ❧ ————

I wanted you to see what real courage is,
instead of getting the idea that courage is
a man with a gun in his hand.
It's when you know you're licked before you begin,
but you begin anyway and see it through
no matter what.

Atticus Finch

Harper Lee, To Kill a Mockingbird

———— ❧ ————

If your experiences would benefit anybody,
give them to someone.

Florence Nightingale

Chapter 22

YOU'RE NOT ALONE: FINDING A SUPPORT GROUP

I will stand with you

When you cannot stand alone

I will fight for you

When all your strength is gone

I will sing for you

So that all can hear your song

Take my hand, lean on me, we will stand.

"We Will Stand," Peter and Gracie Rosenberger

Caregivers suffer from the three "I's": loss of Indepen-dence, loss of Identity, and Isolation. A support group specifically addresses the last two.

In a support group, the caregiver can interact with individuals who share the same feelings and, in many cases, share the same experiences. Support groups allow caregivers the opportunity for community and engagement at their level. The group is a safe place to share frustrations; it's also a great place to learn coping skills and pick up practical tips. In support groups, we can learn how to speak in first-person singular and share our own feelings, dreams, frustrations, heartaches, and even failures.

Support groups often meet at churches, schools, libraries, and other similar public meeting facilities. Whatever issue your loved one is going through, chances are there is a support group. From organizations such as American Cancer Society or the Alzheimer's Association to groups supporting families caring for loved ones with mental health issues, there are so many support groups available. It could be simply a general "caregiver" support group. Regardless, check a couple of them out until you find the one that connects with your circumstances . . . and then stick with it.

> Trouble shared is trouble halved.
>
> *Dorothy Sayers*

Don't look for the perfect support group; rather look for one that strengthens you and engages your heart. You're inserting yourself into a community. You may not like everyone in the group. You may not like the group. By listening and sharing, however, you are working muscles that will better equip you to stay healthy. In addition, don't underestimate how important it is for others to hear your story . . . however painful it may be. A support group engages you as an individual, provides a mechanism for you to grow as a person, and better equips you to endure. The purpose of attending support groups is not to change the issues causing us stress (which we are powerless to change), but rather to help us respond in healthier ways to the extreme challenges we face.

Let us remember therefore this lesson:
That to worship our God sincerely we must
evermore begin by hearkening to His voice,
and by giving ear to what He commands us.
For if every man goes after his own way, we shall wander.

John Calvin

———— ◆ ————

Worship the Lord with gladness.
Come before him, singing with joy.
Acknowledge that the Lord is God!
He made us, and we are his.
We are his people, the sheep of his pasture.

Psalm 100:2–3 NLT

———— ◆ ————

The only thing missing in Ch_rch is "u."

Seen on a Church Sign

Chapter 23

CHURCH: YOU OWE IT
TO YOURSELF

I was glad when they said unto me,
Let us go into the house of the LORD.

Psalm 122:1 KJV

Attending church strengthens our faith and connects us to a loving church body. Isolation is a terrible consequence of caregiving, so connecting with a loving congregation becomes imperative.

As caregivers, attending church each time the doors are open is impossible. The goal is not to put ourselves under some type of system of rules, but rather to help set attainable and realistic targets.

Of course, you are welcome to be an atheist and deal with this stuff, but I don't recommend it. When talking to an atheist, I can't even say, "Good luck with that!" since "luck" implies something other than random chance. So, to any atheists who read this part and reject it, well, "Have at it!"

I advise avoiding "health and wealth" churches that consistently portray God as a Santa-Claus type. These churches have a "vending machine theology"—put money in; make your selection; and get what you want.

Also, I advise that you tune out church folk who tell you they know why your loved ones suffer, or try to give some sort of "consolation" prize such as, "I know what you live with is bad, but look at the good God is doing with it."

> The New Testament does not envisage solitary religion; some kind of regular assembly for worship and instruction is everywhere taken for granted in the Epistles.
>
> *C. S. Lewis*

For the record, I really don't enjoy "consolation conversations." They're just a feeble way of others trying to make sense of something that we're not going to understand this side of heaven. Gracie and I are grateful for the lives our story has touched. Every amputee who receives a limb and walks because of the organization we founded, Standing With Hope, is deeply meaningful to us. But however special those things are, they don't bring us comfort in the dark places. That comfort can only come from the knowledge that God sent His Son to rescue us from a greater tragedy than amputation, surgeries, and pain. Gracie and I both focus on that—rather than trying to wrap ourselves into theological pretzels on the "Why God" questions.

"Why doesn't God heal her?" has caused more insomnia than anything else in my life, and I have yet to rationalize an answer that makes me want to smack my forehead and say, "Ohhhh . . . that's why! I feel better now!"

Given all the hours I've logged with counselors, pastors, and with God, and considering how long I've struggled to understand earthly suffering and God's provision, I am justifiably wary of bombastic individuals who purport to know all the answers, especially if their life isn't filled with brutal challenges.

We're not going to know all the answers until we get to heaven; people who claim to have easy answers to every tragedy are best ignored. (By the way, have you noticed that people who live with great suffering tend to express more humility about "having answers"?)

To strengthen the faith and hearts of caregivers takes a community of believers who humbly minister to each other and reflect Christ into the heartache of this world. Believers who preach and model what God HAS done, versus what He might have done, equip caregivers with solid, substantial, and "grasp-worthy" faith. That church will say, such as Samuel J. Stone preaches:

> The church's one foundation is Jesus Christ her Lord;
> She is his new creation by water and the Word.
> From heaven he came and sought her to be his
>   holy bride;
> with his own blood he bought her, and for her life
>   he died.

"The Church's One Foundation," Samuel J. Stone

When pastors and church leaders point the weary hearts to the Savior, they give them real hope. They walk with them, weep with them, and worship with them.

When a community of believers communicates to me that I am not alone, that God hasn't abandoned me or Gracie, and when they teach me to see the "Purpose-driven Savior," then I am strengthened.

On this side of heaven, I can't speculate on the reasons God does—or doesn't do—things that I simply cannot understand. With the love and support of a group of believers—the church—I can, however, confidently state and rest upon what He HAS done.

Then I can, with countless others, stand and sing:

To God be the glory, great things he hath done!
So loved he the world that he gave us his Son,
who yielded his life an atonement for sin,
and opened the lifegate that all may go in.

"To God Be the Glory," Fanny Crosby

God's got this problem—He thinks He's God!

Dr. Beryl Rosenberger

———◆———

Ignorant kindness may have the effect of cruelty;
but to be angry with it as if it were direct cruelty
would be an ignorant unkindness.

George Eliot

———◆———

Mark out a straight path for your feet;
then stick to the path and stay safe.
Don't get sidetracked. . . .

Proverbs 4:26–27 NLT

Chapter 24

WHY DO FAITH HEALERS
WEAR GLASSES?

*We must speak where the Scripture speaks;
we must keep silent where it is silent.*

John Calvin

Many people living with chronic suffering know from experience that some churches can be hazardous to your faith. Hurting individuals seeking comfort in churches may often encounter those who, when faced with affliction in others, counter it by brandishing the "Sword of the Spirit" like an axe to bludgeon those who are already badly bruised.

Admonishments such as, "If you had enough faith, Jesus would heal you," are not uncommon directives from those poorly educated in biblical teaching: these individuals suffer from a lack of understanding and compassion.

In days past, such doctrinal beliefs and behaviors remained somewhat contained to church circles. Today, however, that message blasts forth on twenty-four-hour cable, social media, and every other type of communication method (some worldwide). And, there seems to be no shortage in mass-media messages promising the next "breakthrough" to those who subscribe to a particular ministry's teachings.

Flipping channels one evening, I happened upon a broadcast of a prominent television evangelist who earned international fame by reporting miraculous healings. Ignoring the carnival-esque atmosphere of the event, my eyes immediately fixed upon the glasses perched on the preacher's nose. *Wait a minute*, I thought to myself. *Doesn't this guy believe that God will heal his poor vision?*

Do minor sufferings such as age-impacted eyesight not qualify for those who bill themselves as having an "anointing-for-healing" ministry? How much suffering is acceptable before traveling to a sawdust-floored tent to hear a man in a white suit pronounce a cure for maladies? To be fair, the tents-and-sawdust shows are now mostly a thing of the past. As the money has rolled in, the new venues-of-choice are indoor arenas with state-of-the-art sound systems and lighting.

The topic of miraculous healing continues to be a flashpoint for people in and out of the church. Of course, the Bible contains many descriptions of healing, prosperity, and comfort. But, a segment of Christianity has hijacked those verses and positioned themselves as authorities on God's provision in relation to the sufferings of this world. The cartoonish behavior of some preachers often serves as fodder for comedians, but there are serious consequences. For those who suffer, the dangling carrot of healing is almost tortuous in itself.

Hurting souls often twist themselves into emotional, spiritual, and financial pretzels as they chase the rainbow of relief. Because they are desperate for healing, sufferers may believe that donating money to a particular ministry is a small price to pay for the alluring offer of God's miraculous provisions. As recently as last week, I heard one well-known minister proclaim on national television that viewers should contribute to his organization because, "God can't work a miracle on our behalf unless we act on faith."

Is that how God works? Is that how the King of kings and Lord of lords ministers to His followers? Should we offer an earnest prayer before plopping down "seed faith" or scratching a Powerball ticket?

When someone we love suffers, we try to help in any way possible. Four friends of a paralytic tore up a roof in order to lower a man down to Jesus while He preached in a crowded house. Since God created us in His own image, would reason not dictate that He feels compassion on an even greater scale than we do?

There is no question that suffering matters to God. How could it not? The Bible gives many examples of the human condition moving God's heart. The Cross stands alone as God's complete and total response to the broken estate of humanity. Furthermore, Scripture teaches that we should continually pray for those afflicted. Clearly, God would not place such directives if He planned to ignore the requests.

Yet it often seems as if our Father remains silent during agonizing days, months, years, or in my family's case—decades. My heart breaks for those who flock to individuals who preach a "rescue you from bad situations" message. I understand the appeal, and I have struggled with the desperation that drives someone to a "miracle crusade." Without any embarrassment, I admit dragging Gracie to a few of those miracle services. Walk a mile in her prosthetic legs before offering criticism.

Living with desperation for this long, however, the panic of finding a solution starts to become tedious. One can only wait for a rescue for so long, before realizing that a life must be lived, even in dire circumstances.

After decades of serving as a "wanna-be-roof-demolisher," I have also heard every type of sales pitch from those who promise relief, often while they fail to see the glaring inconsistency—sometimes perched upon their noses.

God does heal. I state that on faith, after almost three decades as a caregiver—while daily watching Gracie's struggles. I also remain convinced that the resurrection of Christ from the dead trumps any and all miracles. That one event indicates a power sufficient to deal with amputation, pain, and any other calamity. Remaining the bedrock of my faith and conviction, the Cross and the Resurrection continue to place all of the heartache, sadness, despair, and grief into perspective. That conviction is why I feel so passionately about encouraging others to plant themselves in a good church home. And I encourage folks to steer clear of poorly informed folks whose proclamations and advice do more harm than good.

Our strength, our faith, our human connections, and our general well-being improve by attending church. But we must also learn how to respond to those who opine regarding our loved one's condition. Don't feel the need to correct people who consider themselves "instant experts" on the suffering your loved one endures. They don't know better; it's their problem not yours. If, however, your pastor is the one making you feel uncomfortable, find another church.

You're not obligated to listen to ridiculous statements or preposterous propositions, even if those proclamations are made by self-promoters or their acolytes who quote the Bible. In Matthew 7:15, we are warned, "Beware of false prophets, who come to you in sheep's clothing but inwardly are ravenous wolves" (ESV). Trying to explain sense to non-sense is simply not worth it. We can walk away, even while pushing our loved one's wheelchair, without the need to correct others, without feeling guilty—and without feeling rejected by God.

His eye is on the sparrow,
and I know He watches me.

—

Civilla D. Martin

Nobody ever outgrows Scripture;
the book widens and deepens with our years.

C. H. Spurgeon

———◆———

The Holy Scriptures are our letters from home.

St. Augustine

———◆———

"Man shall not live by bread alone,
but by every word that proceeds from the mouth of God."

Matthew 4:4 NKJV

Chapter 25

THY WORD IS A LAMP
UNTO MY FEET

Every word of God proves true;
he is a shield to those who take refuge in him.

Proverbs 30:5 ESV

The Bible doesn't lay out every answer to every question, nor does it cover every tragic scenario. What it does do, however, is clearly describe in great detail a sovereign, all-wise, loving God who bore the entire stench and judgment of man's sin upon His own Son. That same God weaves HIS purpose into even the most horrific circumstances, and one day we will see it made plain before us. When we do, every knee will bow and every tongue confess that Jesus Christ is Lord.

That knowledge has sustained uncounted millions through brutal realities and can sustain caregivers, as well.

Given that, churches are still filled with broken people, and even the best of churches will have dysfunction. A flawed church doesn't excuse our absence, but caregivers (and others) would benefit from using great wisdom when selecting a church. I make it a rule to avoid church folks who do the following:

- Talk a lot about "getting something from God," instead of focusing on what we've already received.

- Seem to have an answer for everything, which usually involves "something you have to do better."

- Spend more time talking about "getting your breakthrough" rather than focusing on the need for repentance, and trusting God's provision—even in suffering.

- Preach sermons that would make better self-help speeches. I like motivational seminars as much as the next guy, but sermons need to preach the gospel, the plan of salvation, and point to Christ.

Motivational messages don't hold up in the long run. The Gospel, however, sustains through all the pain and hardship the world can dish out. Rather than hopping around to find someone to give us the next "feel-good" and motivational-evangelical gimmick, we seek out companionship and fellowship—and develop relationships that build us up with sustainable truth.

God's plan and purpose in all of this is greater than our understanding. We are caregivers, not consultants. Focusing on what God DID do that we CAN understand, however, helps strengthen our faith and bolster courage. I know that one day I'll be in heaven with Him . . . and all of my questions will be answered. In the meantime, I choose to hang on to what Paul said in his epistle to the Romans:

> *And we know that all things work together for good to those who love God to those who are called according to His purpose.*
>
> *Romans 8:28 NKJV*

God has given us the Bible for the purpose of knowing His promises, His power, His commandments, His wisdom, His love, and His Son. As we study God's teachings and apply them to our lives, we live by the Word that shall never pass away.

Hearty laughter is a good way to jog internally
without having to go outdoors.

Norman Cousins

Laughter is the sun that drives winter
from the human face.

Victor Hugo

I met the surgeon general.
He offered me a cigarette.

Rodney Dangerfield

Laughter gives us distance.
It allows us to step back from an event,
deal with it, and then move on.

Bob Newhart

Chapter 26

———— ❧ ————

LAUGH WHEN YOU CAN

*The person who can bring the spirit of laughter
into a room is indeed blessed.*

Bennett Cerf

Jeff Foxworthy and I came up with a video clip for AARP.
It was called, "You Might Be a Caregiver If . . ." Here are
a few highlights:

Peter: "If you have ever changed a dressing while cooking
turkey and dressing, you might be a caregiver."

Jeff: "If you have ever hooked up your dog to your wife's
wheelchair, just to see if it would work . . . you might
be a caregiver."

Peter: "If you've ever used Neosporin as a verb, you're probably a caregiver."

Jeff: "Do it …"

Peter: "Hold still, baby, I gotta Neosporin this so we can get to church on time."

Jeff: "If anyone has ever seriously asked you, 'Baby, have you seen my left leg?'"

Peter: (Doubled over laughing and can't speak!).

———◆———

Although humor sometimes serves as a bit of a shield to stave off painful feelings, genuinely funny moments in even the direst of circumstances continue to surprise (and delight) me.

I once heard a story about a beloved church leader from a small, rural congregation who passed away following a long illness. As a tribute and gift to the widow, the music minister offered to enlist the choir to sing the man's favorite song at the funeral. Inquiring from the bereaved woman, the music minister was surprised to hear that the dearly departed's favorite song was "Jingle Bells."

Double-checking with her, she emphatically stated that his favorite song was indeed "Jingle Bells" and expressed great gratitude that the choir offered to sing her deceased husband's much-loved song at the service.

So the music minister assembled the choir, and, with sales skills rivaling the best salesman on the planet, convinced the church choir to perform "Jingle Bells" at the funeral, which took place in June.

After the eulogy, the choir stood up and belted out, "Dashing through the snow, in a one-horse open sleigh . . ."

As the assembled crowd of family and friends looked on with puzzlement, while dressed in summer attire, the embarrassed, but committed, choir sat down feeling as if they did the best they could for the grieving widow.

At the graveside, the music minister passed by the man's wife, took her hand, and once again gave his sincere condolences. Tearfully thanking him for the music, she quizzically looked at the music minister and remarked, "I loved all the hymns and songs, but why did you all sing 'Jingle Bells'?

Wide-eyed, the music minister replied, "You stated it was his favorite song."

With a sad, but sweet, grin she put her hand to her mouth and laughed. "Ohhhh, I am so sorry. I meant, 'Golden Bells'!"

———··———

Sometimes humor meets tragedy in strange places. Our challenge is to expect and enjoy it.

Over the years I've met quite a few comedians, and each of them makes a living seeing often painful issues through "funny-shaped" lenses. As a writer, I try to incorporate as much humor and wit as possible in all I write. People often ask me who inspires me as a writer. I usually enthusiastically state, "Lewis!" With admiration and raised eyebrows, many cerebral types respond, "C. S.?"

"No . . . Grizzard!"

In certain circles, my reply usually results in confused or disappointed faces, but I discovered two kinds of people: those who like Lewis Grizzard and those who don't know any better.

———··———

With a vast spectrum of comedic tastes to choose from, pick one that makes your sides split. Seinfeld to Foxworthy, Andy Griffith to Tim Allen; a host of comedians compete for our amusement, so let's take them up on it! Watch a funny movie, catch a stand-up comedian on television, or read a hilarious author. When you do, you'll feel the stress melt off your heart.

Caregiving is serious business, but life can be whimsical; go with it and lighten up a bit.

If you ever start feeling like you have the goofiest, craziest,

most dysfunctional family in the world,

all you have to do is go to a state fair.

Because five minutes at the fair, you'll be going,

"You know, we're alright.

We are dang near royalty."

Jeff Foxworthy

People who cannot find time for recreation
are obliged sooner or later to find time for illness.

John Wannamaker

———◆———

A happy heart makes the face cheerful,
but heartache crushes the spirit.

Proverbs 15:13 NIV

Chapter 27

───⋘❈⋙───

YOU ARE NOW FREE
TO GET UP AND MOVE
AROUND . . .

Lighten up while you still can; don't even try to understand.
Just find a place to make your stand and take it easy.

The Eagles, Glenn Frey/Jackson Browne

Lighten up. Have some fun. Take a well-deserved break.
You'll be doing yourself *and* your loved one a favor.

Sometimes it is possible to have fun with the person you
are caring for, but most of the time, even the "fun things"
become work for caregivers who have to help their loved ones
have fun.

I don't need over-the-top entertainment. I'm pretty
good with a Louis L'Amour western, and, truthfully, of all
the caregivers I've met in my life, 100% of them just want a

quiet, restful place to be alone with their thoughts without having to worry about someone else.

When I get a break, I feel time slows down for me. When on the road, I don't mind the travel, especially when I'm not taking care of another person. The TSA seems nicer, airplane food (what little there is now days) tastes better, the sunsets are prettier, the birds sing more, and the list goes on. It's not that I am happier per se. It's that I slow down and enjoy the little things and the quiet moments.

The abilities and stability of caregivers increase with regular rest and leisure. Even God took a Sabbath rest. Free time means just that: *free* time. We must relax and improve our state of mind and body. Wrapping our entire beings into our role as caregivers taxes the love we have for our charges and saps our identity, our creativity, and our ability to focus.

When we slow down long enough to make time for life's simple pleasures, everybody wins. So, what are you waiting for?

———◆———

Adapt yourself to the things among which
your lot has been cast and love sincerely
the fellow creatures with whom destiny has
ordained that you shall live.

—

Marcus Aurelius

———◆———

We are all here for a spell,
get all the good laughs you can.

Will Rogers

———————

First pay attention to me, and then relax.
Now you can take it easy—you're in good hands.

Proverbs 1:33 MSG

Chapter 28

LEAVE

You deserve a break today. So get up and get away . . .

Advertising Slogan for McDonald's

Honestly, we have to get some space. It doesn't have to be at McDonald's necessarily, but we caregivers need to get away on a regular basis.

For the first forty surgeries Gracie endured under my watch, I used to stay nearly around the clock with her at the hospital.

Big mistake.

Before we married, Gracie underwent her twenty-first surgery, but it was the first one with me. Although newly engaged, I had not yet "gotten my feet wet" as a caregiver, and several family members watched me to see how I would handle the pressure. The surgeon met with the family following the procedure and assured everyone that she was fine but would be in recovery for some time. Breathing a sigh of relief, we all smiled at each other, until I did the unthinkable: I went to a movie to blow off some steam and relax.

I later learned of the gasps and disapproval by some of those gathered around. One of them was a relative of a relative, and had no "skin in the game," but she felt it her duty to properly evaluate my behavior and hold up a scorecard as if she served as an Olympic judge during a diving contest.

It didn't help that she was also a "holier than thou" type. You know the ones: They have a bumper sticker on their Cadillac that states "My Other Car Is a Chariot of Fire!"

While I took a break and enjoyed myself at the movie, the judgment piled higher, as the group seemed to revel in how I "just wasn't up to the task."

A friend pulled me aside to share all this with me, and I mistakenly acted contrite to get into good graces with everyone. My instincts, however, were exactly right. Gracie had a whole team of nurses and doctors *at the hospital*. She needed me *after* those professionals were no longer available.

For a one-time event like a broken arm or something, this "get-away" principle doesn't necessarily apply. Issues stretching over years, however, are "game changers."

So, when help is present, take advantage of it by leaving the premises and allowing fresh air into your body and soul. Caregivers require regular breaks, preferably without being criticized by others.

While I'm at it, I developed a policy about people who criticize how I handle caregiving issues and the decisions I make as a caregiver: *The length of time I will listen to someone criticize is in direct proportion to how much time the critic spends helping.*

If you like that policy, you are welcome to use it, and I hope it helps stave off those who simply want to gripe.

When managing your lifestyle, the three "L's" become an easy tool to remind yourself to take it easy: "LAUGH, LEISURE, LEAVE." So, here's a **1-2-30 reminder.**

1: Do at least one special thing for yourself each week.

Catch a movie, golf, go to a museum, ride your bike, go fishing, or find something else you enjoy. Do one special something for yourself every week. Sometimes I like catching a movie or a good book, but other times I find myself alone in the sanctuary at our church playing the piano for an hour or two.

If you need someone to sit with your loved one while you take a break, call your church. If your church won't help with that, ask a friend (and then change churches).

2: Take at least two weeks' annual vacation from caregiving each year.

You probably can't take fourteen days off in a row, but by spreading it over the year, it becomes possible. It's roughly a day and a night off every month. Yes, it may mean asking for help from others. That's where the church offers great assistance.

Church leaders can help find a person who can help, or even find the funds to pay for skilled care of some type (RN, LPN), or work with a local caregiver respite organization to provide someone to stay overnight while you get out of town for a night or so.

Most services that offer something like that run around $15–20 per hour (depending upon location). Although that sounds like a lot of money, there are ways around the costs.

The challenge for caregivers is to make the commitment to care for themselves, and then watch the resources appear. Experience teaches me that it's not a lack of resources but a lack of resourcefulness that prohibits progress.

Churches are full of professionals, students, young people, retired members, and so forth, who can volunteer. Most caregivers have some sort of family structure to help share the load, but for those who do not, a church family becomes imperative. It is important for the church to bring its considerable resources to the table by helping with extreme caregiver situations, such as single mothers with a special needs child, elderly spouses caring for each other, one person dealing with a catastrophic illness over lengthy periods of time, etc.

It's not enough to simply write a check. The goal is sustainability for the caregiver—and that often means developing a professional plan, as well. Churches are equipped with business and community leaders who can provide that type of counsel to those single parents/young families with special needs children or those at middle-age struggling to balance work with caregiving. Avoid sending a check; instead, develop a plan.

30: Take at least thirty minutes a day to enjoy something humorous.

Television is full of sitcoms (some of them stupid; others profane and disgusting), but somewhere in all of that programming, there are laughs waiting for you. Go get them. If television is not your thing, load comics onto your iPod and listen to them while going for a walk, and kill two birds with one stone (or, like Chuck Norris, you can kill two stones with one bird!).

For the frugal, your local library has all kinds of things just waiting for you to check them out! Find something that makes you laugh for thirty minutes a day! I download to my phone a free app of jokes that just make me cry with laughter. Granted, amusing me is not difficult, but the benefit is a better disposition and a little lighter outlook. Everyone has a sense of humor, but caregivers may require a bit more help cultivating theirs.

Caregiving is hard, wearisome work—you deserve an occasional break from the daily grind. With these few ideas, you can inject a lot of sunshine and fresh air into a dreary situation. By doing so, the one you love benefits from a healthy caregiver—and you as the caregiver give yourself permission to live a more meaningful and joyful life.

———◆———

Laughter is to life what
shock absorbers are to automobiles.
It won't take the potholes out of the road,
but it sure makes the ride smoother.

—

Barbara Johnson

———◆———

You can easily judge the character of a man by
how he treats those who can do nothing for him.

Johann Wolfgang von Goethe

There never was any heart truly great and generous,
that was not also tender and compassionate.

Robert Frost

Chapter 29

SEPARATE THE PERSON FROM THE PAIN

Beyond all these things put on love,
which is the perfect bond of unity.

Colossians 3:14 NASB

How do you keep love and passion thriving in a chronic medical catastrophe where the suffering is not limited to a short-term illness or injury?

Different from Alzheimer's or dementia, couples impacted by one spouse's living with a broken or diseased body while retaining complete cognitive awareness presents a different set of emotional trials for the marriage. The challenge for the healthy spouse is to maneuver through the minefield of medical issues, attending to each of them, but never losing sight of the suffering person's heart. Taking care of the body does not always equate to caring for the heart.

The challenge for the sick or injured spouse, even from a wheelchair—or while experiencing severe chronic pain—is to recognize that matters of the heart, though often less demanding, are just as important (if not more so) as the needs of the body.

If I'm laden at all
I'm laden with sadness
That everyone's heart
Isn't filled with the gladness
Of love for one another.

"He Ain't Heavy, He's My Brother"
Bobby Scott and Bob Russell

If your loved one is suffering from a life-altering condition, it's imperative that you separate the person from the pain. Doing so is difficult but not impossible. With lots of practice, plenty of prayer, help from those who will give it, and consistent encouragement from trusted counselors, you'll keep reminding yourself that the person you're caring for is much more than a name on a chart.

Son, daughter, parent, spouse, sibling, cousin, friend— a person, not a patient. Their challenges *belong* to them but are *not* them. Although my wife is missing both legs, she is defined by so much more than the sum or lack of body parts. By looking beyond disabilities and deformities, we release ourselves from a previously unknown bondage of judging others by a faulty standard of normal.

That newfound freedom enables us to love with precision—right to the heart. In doing so, we discover priceless moments of joy in the relationship, even if they can't respond to us in a way that we desire. Recognizing the inexhaustible source of love flowing from God frees us to unreservedly pour love into others.

A man who gives in to temptation after
five minutes simply does not know
what it would have been like an hour later.

C. S. Lewis

———◆◆———

The grace of God is the one thing we cannot do
without in this life or in the life to come;
it has no substitutes, artificial, temporary, or otherwise.

Bill Bright

———◆◆———

You lay your bets and then you pay the price
The things we do for love, the things we do for love.

"The Things We Do for Love," 10 CC

Graham Gouldman/Eric Stewart

Chapter 30

WHEN EMOTIONS TURN SELF-DESTRUCTIVE

Be sober, be vigilant; because your adversary the devil walks
about like a roaring lion, seeking whom he may devour.

1 Peter 5:8 NKJV

Over-stressed caregivers may convince themselves that they've earned the right to "blow off a little steam." I know. I've been there, thought that, done that, and got the scars to prove it.

I had to learn the hard way that strong emotions, combined with unrelenting stress and sheer exhaustion, make a dangerous mix.

Here in the twenty-first century, temptations are completely and thoroughly woven into the fabric of everyday life. So, unless you're a hermit living on a deserted island without

WiFi, you'll probably be tempted by somebody or something *today*—in fact, you will probably be tempted on countless occasions. Why? Because you live in a world that's filled to the brim with temptations and addictions that can lead you far, far away from your family, your faith, your personal responsibilities, and your Maker.

Like the old saying goes, "The price of freedom is eternal vigilance." If you're always vigilant, you can stay out of the trap; if you let down your guard, you may get snared.

Caregivers can't effectively live and serve others if they're carrying around massive loads of guilt and shame. So what are we, as mere mortals, to do when we fall short? The answer, in my opinion, is summed up in a five-letter word: G-R-A-C-E.

By constantly reminding ourselves that God's grace covers our sins (not so we have a license to keep repeating them), we discover that guilt no longer whips us into a frenzy. Grace frees us to love and to serve from a clean heart.

From experience I know the agony of trying to serve as a caregiver while maintaining a life filled with destructive coping mechanisms. To be clear, the challenges of caregiving don't cause character defects, they only amplify them—and can act like "Miracle Grow" for our faults. When those faults lead caregivers to cope using sex, alcohol, drugs, or other addictions, these harmful "escapes" always lead down a destructive path.

We live in a fallen, broken world where bad things happen, often without a fairy-tale ending. That won't change until Christ returns. And, if you want to navigate your way safely through that fallen world, you'll guard yourself against the misplaced emotions and the self-destructive behaviors that are tearing our families and our society apart.

You can't be perfect. But there are several things you *can* do. Seeing a counselor once a month and support groups twice a month, calling a close friend or pastor regularly that you can trust with your weakness and weariness; these are ways that you can push back against temptations.

Whatever "relief" that's "promised" by various coping mechanisms—such as illicit sexual activity, illicit emotional activity, drugs, or alcohol—is a lie that will rip you apart.

You don't have to take my word for it; you're certainly free to chart your own path.

But as someone who's made virtually every mistake one can make on this journey, I don't recommend it. I've found it wise to listen to people with a lot of scars. Their experience can help me avoid the injuries they've endured.

Life is not always what one wants it to be,

but to make the best of it, as it is,

is the only way of being happy.

Jenny Jerome Churchill

———— ·•·•· ————

We deem those happy who, from the experience of life,

have learned to bear its ills,

without being overcome by them.

Juvenal

———— ·•·•· ————

There are two ways of meeting difficulties:

You alter the difficulties, or you alter yourself to meet them.

Phyllis Bottome

Chapter 31

———— ❧ ————

KEEP LIVING,
EVEN WHILE HURTING

Live the life you are given as well as you can.

Cardinal Joseph Bernadine

It is appropriate to acknowledge our hurts. But, after nearly three decades of living with someone who daily suffers from severe chronic pain, I have witnessed the difference between "living with pain" versus "living while in pain." My wife didn't have to go to Africa and launch a prosthetic limb ministry. She could have easily chosen to focus on herself and her own challenges. She purposed, however, to give out of her lack—and in doing so, she continues to touch a great many lives even though she currently has limited travel. She saw something worthwhile that did not reduce her pain but rather transcended it. The lesson I learned from her is:

it's possible and rewarding to live a full and rich life while in pain.

We don't have to wait until we "feel good" before we participate in life. And, we don't have to wait until we're "healthy" before we succeed. I remember a special night in Madison Square Garden right after President George W. Bush gave his acceptance speech for the nomination in 2004. Invited to be on the platform behind the President following Gracie's performance at the convention two nights prior, we had to be in place on the stage early in the evening. For several hours we sat there, while my wife's pain levels escalated. She knew she would be uncomfortable, and she knew it would be a long night, but we lived in the moment together, and after the President left, we danced together among the fallen balloons and confetti while country singer Lee Ann Womack stood just feet away singing her hit song, "I Hope You Dance."

Gracie did opt to forgo wearing dress shoes in order to be a bit more comfortable. You can still see us in pictures sitting just behind the President's left shoulder. Gracie's robotic-looking legs are in plain view with her bright white sneakers, which I think is hilarious! If Gracie and the President of the United States didn't mind, no one else should!

If we wait until we feel good or until things are "going our way" before we choose to engage in life, we are missing out on undiscovered joy and deeply rewarding moments— we're missing out on life.

We're as miserable or happy as we choose to be.

———

And when you get the choice to sit it out or dance.

I hope you dance.

"I Hope You Dance"

Mark D. Sanders/Tia Sillers

PART IV

❖

PLANNING

The plans of the diligent lead surely to plenty.

Proverbs 21:5 NKJV

A danger foreseen is half avoided.

Thomas Fuller

Life is about not knowing, having to change,
taking the moment and making the best of it,
without knowing what's going to happen next.

Gilda Radner

Crisis brings us face to face with our inadequacy
and our inadequacy in turn leads us
to the inexhaustible sufficiency of God.

Catherine Marshall

Chapter 32

CRISIS MANAGEMENT IS
AN OXYMORON

There cannot be a crisis next week.
My schedule is already full.

Henry Kissinger

Caregiving not only affects the caregiver's health and emotions but also their lifestyle.

- 20 hours per week is the average number of hours family caregivers spend attending to their loved ones.
- 13% of family caregivers are providing 40 hours of care a week or more.

With responsibilities like these, you can forget trying to plan a vacation; it's usually a major event just to go to see a movie!

Starting out each morning anticipating the "crisis du jour," we caregivers frequently throw our hands up in exasperation at trying to schedule and reschedule things. With the daily bombardment of medical and caregiving issues, is it possible to carve out some things to improve our overall well-being? It doesn't require a trip to Italy or an exotic island beach. Is it too much to ask for a quiet cot in the corner with no one bothering us for a couple of hours?!

In the context of caregiving, feeling better about ourselves is not a selfish and egocentric pursuit. A more relaxed, self-confident, and emotionally calm caregiver almost guarantees that his/her charge will receive better and more consistent care. If the loved one is not cognitively impaired, the relationship can even deepen when a caregiver feels rested and refreshed.

I can't give you precise solutions to the crises you'll face. But what I can promise you is the following:

- Every crisis will eventually pass.
- You'll be better equipped to weather the crisis if you've already created a support system that includes a church, a counselor, and a support group.

- You'll be better equipped to face tomorrow's crisis if you take care of yourself today.

Every caregiver needs time off, but fear, obligation, and guilt (FOG) often shelve breaks. Getting away is not easy, and it may have to be in small but consistent chunks of time. Carving out "downtime" is paramount to serving as a good caregiver. I know your loved one suffers—so does mine—but you and I can't change that fact, nor will we help them by driving ourselves until we're nothing but a husk.

Nothing in the world can take the place of persistence.
Talent will not; genius will not; education will not.
Persistence and determination alone are omnipotent.

Calvin Coolidge

I walk slowly, but I never walk backwards.

Abraham Lincoln

About all I ever did was stick with it.

Bear Bryant

This is the day the LORD has made;
we will rejoice and be glad in it.

Psalm 118:24 NKJV

Make each day your masterpiece.

John Wooden

Chapter 33

❦

CAREGIVING,
ONE DAY AT A TIME

The most important history is the history we make today.

Henry Ford

Caregiving is one of the toughest jobs on planet Earth. It's a job that almost nobody can do for a lifetime but anyone can do for twenty-four hours. What's required is patience, a willingness to do each day's work as it comes, and a commitment to focus on today's work, not the worries of tomorrow.

Robert Louis Stevenson could have been talking directly to caregivers when he wrote:

> Anyone can carry his burden, however hard, until nightfall. Anyone can do his work, however hard,

179

for one day. Anyone can live sweetly, patiently, lovingly, purely, till the sun goes down. And this is all that life really means.

Every day presents its own set of challenges and opportunities. Yesterday's opportunities are gone forever, and tomorrow's may never come. It's okay to look backwards but don't stare. The future is beyond my control as well. But today's opportunities are very real and, because you're a caregiver, critical to the well-being of your loved one.

Today, because you're a caregiver, you can make a positive impact on the life of another human being.

Today, because you're a caregiver, you can make your corner of the world a better place.

Today, because you're a caregiver, you can be a living, breathing example of what it means to be a true servant.

Today, you can share God's love through a smile, a hug, a kind word, or a heartfelt prayer.

Yesterday? That's over and done. It's a cancelled check.

Tomorrow? That's God's business—and He will provide the courage and wisdom to deal with it when it arrives.

So, that leaves only a single solitary day that's available for our use. Here's how Jesus said it should be used:

—————◆◆◆—————

But seek first his kingdom and his righteousness,
and all these things will be given to you as well.
Therefore do not worry about tomorrow,
for tomorrow will worry about itself.
Each day has enough trouble of its own.

Matthew 6:33–34 NIV

—————◆◆◆—————

"In quietness and trust is your strength."

Isaiah 30:15 NASB

------◆------

The best remedy for those who are afraid,
lonely or unhappy is to go outside, somewhere where
they can be quite alone with the heavens, nature and God.

Anne Frank

------◆------

Be still, my soul: the Lord is on thy side.
Bear patiently the cross of grief or pain.
Leave to thy God to order and provide;
In every change, He faithful will remain.
Be still, my soul: thy best, thy heavenly Friend
Through thorny ways leads to a joyful end.

"Be Still My Soul," Katharina von Schlegel

------◆------

I wait quietly before God, for my hope is in him.

Psalm 62:5 NLT

Chapter 34

＊＊＊

MAKING TIME
FOR QUIET TIME

Here's a gift you give yourself. Sometime in your day today,
try to turn off all the noises you can around you,
and give yourself some quiet time.

Fred Rogers

Here's a simple little prescription for becoming a better caregiver: carve out some quiet time every day. In our noisy, twenty-first-century world, silence is highly underrated. Many of us can't even seem to walk from the front door to the street without a cell phone or an iPod in our ear. The world seems to grow louder day by day, and our senses seem to be invaded at every turn.

If we allow the distractions of this clamorous society to totally envelope our days, we do ourselves a profound disservice. Being still takes practice. The first time you try it, you may fall asleep. Good. Try it again the next day. Frantic people make frantic decisions. Someone in your life is counting on you to make good ones. Would you trust your well-being to someone who stays frazzled?

Rather than spending our entire days glued to our electronic devices, we're wise to carve out a few moments for quiet reflection. When we do, we are rewarded and so are the ones we care for.

Are you too busy to grab a few minutes of quiet time each day? If so, it's probably time to rearrange your to-do list. I've found that if I don't take time for stillness, I'll have to make time for illness.

As a caregiver, it's your responsibility to stay emotionally healthy. Quiet time helps you stay that way. But don't take my word for it. Just ask Mr. Rogers.

That's why I'm easy
I'm easy like Sunday morning.

"Easy Like Sunday Morning"
Lionel Richie, The Commodores

A hospital bed is a parked taxi with the meter running.

Groucho Marx

———✦———

Money is a terrible master but an excellent servant.

P. T. Barnum

———✦———

I have enough money to last me the rest of my life,
unless I buy something.

Jackie Mason

Chapter 35

ADDING MONEY CHALLENGES TO THE MIX

The wise see danger ahead and avoid it. . . .

Proverbs 22:3 NCV

Caregiving is challenging enough, but adding money issues to the mix creates a massive strain on individuals and families. Three decades of caregiving experience leads me to believe that, although they may help, I cannot permanently rely on a government program, an individual, a family member, or a lottery ticket to come to my rescue. *By the way, the lottery is simply a tax on people who are bad at math.*

What I am sure of is this: Caregiving requires long hours, weary nights, and constant battles to stretch a dollar until it is translucent.

From a server struggling to make tips working at a restaurant while caring for a sick spouse, to multimillionaire children able to pay for full-time care for aging parents, I've encountered individuals in virtually every type of caregiving situation. Most of us fall somewhere in the middle, but we lean toward the server trying to squeeze out a living.

- Caregiving families (families in which one member has a disability) have median incomes that are more than 15% lower than non-caregiving families. In every state the poverty rate is higher among families with members with a disability than among families without.

- During the 2009 economic downturn, one in five family caregivers had to move into the same home with their loved ones to cut expenses.

- 47% of working caregivers indicate an increase in caregiving expenses has caused them to use up all or most of their savings.

- The average family caregiver for someone fifty years or older spent $5,531 per year on out-of-pocket caregiving expenses in 2007, which was more than 10% of the median income for a family caregiver that year.

Many financial experts share strategies for dealing with money, getting out of debt, and saving for retirement, yet

I've not heard one of them who has even remotely juggled anything like my family's three decades of surgeries, pain, constant crises, and health costs (cresting $9 million). Here are a few of the dilemmas I've pondered over the years:

- What kind of financial impact will the illness have on our family's budget?
- How does this affect my ability to pay my bills, realize professional potential and earn more, prepare for retirement, have peace of mind, or tithe to my church?
- How do I keep my head above water?
- Is it possible to "get ahead"?

These questions (and many more) serve as the regular topics during my frequent late-night conversations with the ceiling fan.

Before launching my radio show and writing my book, *Wear Comfortable Shoes: Surviving and Thriving as a Caregiver*, I spent a great deal of time thinking about this: What does "help" look like to a caregiver? For example, having someone bring meals to the family is helpful, but eventually someone has to learn to cook.

Likewise with money: A gift of cash in time of need

is helpful. Ultimately, however, one must earn a living and effectively manage money.

The key is sustainability, and in order to manage the massive bills, extra costs, and nuances of the tax code, I have found that I need the help of trained professionals— specifically certified public accountants (CPA).

I look at a CPA almost like a primary care doctor. To me, the CPA functions as the "hub" of the financial wheel of life. From mortgages to tax deductions, a CPA can serve as a guide through the financial jungle of both individual budgets and our national economy. When my heating unit needs servicing, I leave it to the professionals. When my financial "unit" needs servicing, I also call the professionals.

How many accountants does it take to change a light bulb?
Hmmm . . . I'll just do a few numbers and get back to you!

How can you tell when an accountant is on vacation?
He shows up at 8:30 a.m.

The Accountant's Prayer
Lord, help me become more flexible . . .
Starting tomorrow morning at 7:59 a.m. CST

I won't presume to tell anyone, particularly caregivers, how to manage their money. I can offer another **1-2-30 reminder** that changed the way I view money, helped me keep a superior credit rating and avoid bankruptcy while dealing with the massive medical bills incurred for the last several decades.

- Find one charity that has nothing to do with your situation that you can regularly support. It may be only $5 per month, but I find it helpful to make a positive difference into someone else's life and not be consumed with my own.

- Make sure you see your financial counselor at least twice a year to ensure that budgets are met, taxes are filed, and there is some sustainable plan. Since it is inconsistent to call yourself a caregiver if you don't have life insurance, make one of those visits with a financial planner.

- Sock $30 per paycheck into some sort of savings/rainy day fund. Some can do $30,000, but most of us can't. Do what you can but try to hit at least $30 per paycheck.

You have power over your mind—not outside events.
Realize this, and you will find strength.

Marcus Aurelius, Meditations

———◦◦◦———

Not being able to govern events, I govern myself.

Michel de Montaigne

Chapter 36

ABOUT INSURANCE,
DOCTORS,
AND THE SYSTEM

These should learn first of all to put their religion
into practice by caring for their own family. . . .

1 Timothy 5:4 NIV

As a caregiver, you need insurance—not just medical. In fact, consider how important life insurance is to your loved one. Don't assume you will outlive that loved one simply because they are elderly, disabled, or chronically ill. If you don't have life insurance and something happens to before your loved one, you've wasted all your blood, sweat, and treasure as a caregiver by leaving them without resources—*and* without a caregiver. Purchasing life insurance may stretch you financially, but with the help of a good financial planner, it's not really that complicated.

Health Care is complicated. Heath insurance, not so much. I can attest, however, that while the healthcare system is complex, it's not impossible to navigate. One quick tip; I've never heard of any property insurance company selling a policy on a car after the wreck. If you postpone getting health insurance because you're not currently sick, you're playing Russian roulette, and, quite truthfully, you're part of the problem in our country.

After countless explanations of benefits (EOB) from now seven different insurance companies covering an immense amount of procedures and medical needs, I have never lost an appeal.

From nurses to surgeons, I have confronted, managed, appealed to, and recruited more medical professionals to my viewpoint than I can recall. I treat each of them with deference but not subservience.

Each professional who cares for my wife receives a paycheck; I do not. Volunteering does not make me special, but I am different. My stake in the journey is unlike those who do it for a living. My status as a spouse also places me in a category distinct from relatives who volunteer. I remain the only person in Gracie's life not connected by blood or money who has willingly chosen to care for her in this manner.

Understanding the role and motivation of an individual better equips you to speak to the core issue and need. A child caring for a parent will have different needs than a sibling or spouse caregiver. A medical professional will also have a different sort of needs. Saying that they're just doing it for a paycheck is a cop-out. There's an underlying reason why they chose this profession. When negotiating with them, learn and speak to that reason. That's how you move the ball down the field as an advocate.

While I cannot give you a comprehensive guide to every health insurance issue, here are a few things I've learned along the way.

Be polite, but don't grovel: As you navigate through the healthcare system, angry words rarely help the situation. But neither does subservience. So don't scream and shout. But if you know you're right, stand your ground. Say what you mean, mean what you say . . . but don't say it mean.

Remember that when it comes to your loved one, you're an expert too: As I shared with one surgeon recently, "With all due respect, Doctor, I've cared for Gracie since you were in junior high school—*and I know what I'm talking about.*"

Keep good records: I know record-keeping is a pain, and I understand that it's hard to keep up with the inevitable mountains of paperwork. But it's necessary. When the time comes to make your case, you need to be fully informed not completely confused. I scan and keep them electronically, and everything is backed up. I don't have room in my office for the volume of data Gracie generates.

Don't be intimidated: The healthcare system is big, but you and your loved one still have rights. If you think your claims are valid, don't be afraid to say so loudly and often.

Dress appropriately: Face it, who would you defer to: a man in a suit with a groomed appearance or a guy in cut-offs and in a Van Halen T-shirt?

Practice speaking: Ask someone you trust to verify whether or not you butcher the Queen's English. I don't make the rules, but if you come across like a rube, people will treat you like one. Shakespeare said, "Brevity is the soul of wit." Condense your thoughts into the smallest ideas, concepts, and questions so that you get right to the heart of the issue without the drama, stammering, or wasting of time because you didn't do your due diligence. I had a prepared ninety-second speech I once gave to a doctor. I practiced it while driving, working around the house, etc. When the appointment came, I delivered. And I won.

Practice writing: It is always a good idea to write out things for each doctor visit. Go back and edit if needed.

Get a case worker: When dealing with a long-term chronic illness/disability, your medical insurance should have a case-worker they can assign to you. For many years, ours was an RN named Paul, who was simply a GREAT guy. He and I talked often and became good friends. He developed a strong grasp of Gracie's injuries and needs, provided great leadership to me, and served as a friendly liaison to the insurance company. A case worker from your loved one's medical insurance company will save you time, headache, heartache, and even money.

Care advocate: When negotiating with an insurance company, if you feel like David against Goliath, you're not alone—and don't try to do it alone. There are companies that provide patient care advocates. This service becomes hugely helpful if your loved one lives in a different town. Usually a nurse or similarly trained professional, they work for you, not the insurance company, hospital, or physician. They can fight (and win) battles that you just may be too weary or unable to engage.

What to bring to a fight: Sometimes, you will be at odds with your insurance company—it happens, but don't panic. I don't appeal to the humanity of insurance companies (it's a corporation not a person), nor do I argue with them with a Bible in one hand and the US Constitution in the other. Through math, I am able to demonstrate how it's in their best interest to cover a particular drug or procedure (make sure it is!)

To paraphrase the old saying about going to a fight, "If they bring a knife, I'll bring a calculator." Math wins every time.

———

I remember sitting in the critical-care family waiting area once and noticed a man standing helplessly in the middle of the room, twisting his cap. Wearing work boots and dressed as if he stepped right off the farm, this frightened man looked completely out of his element.

Evaluating his clothing, I surmised that in his world, he was most likely extremely capable around heavy machinery, possibly livestock. In his world, he was an expert.

But he was no longer in his world. In the world he now found himself, people dressed strangely, talked in codes and different languages, moved at light speed, and days and nights often ran together. Beeping, screaming, constant pages on the intercom, unfamiliar sights and smells—think about the shock of the harsh new environment, and then add that to the worry and fear over his loved one lying in critical care.

This is the world we caregivers live in, and we must adapt. Otherwise, we will be at the mercy of that world until it chews us and our loved ones up.

In that critical area waiting room, I decided that, although I couldn't control it, I also wouldn't be at the mercy of that world.

You don't have to, either.

"But as for you, be strong and do not give up, for your work will be rewarded."

2 Chronicles 15:7 NIV

———⊰•⊱———

Do Lipton employees take coffee breaks?

Steven Wright

Chapter 37

YOUR OTHER CAREER

If I do my full duty, the rest will take care of itself.

George S. Patton

According to a 2009 study conducted by the National Alliance for Caregiving in collaboration with AARP, approximately "73% of family caregivers who care for someone over the age of eighteen either work or have worked while providing care." With 65 million Americans serving as volunteer caregivers for vulnerable loved ones, it's clear that a vast number of today's workers are saddled with the extra responsibilities of caregiving. And with baby boomers racing into senior status, tomorrow's workforce will find itself struggling to care for a huge population of aging parents.

The alarm bells are sounding: A large number of individuals will require volunteer caregivers, and the trend clearly reveals that more and more workers will need to juggle their professional lives while caring for their loved ones.

MetLife provided a 2010 study that showed American workers from every profession are struggling to balance work responsibilities while serving as caregivers. The MetLife report revealed significantly higher costs to the employer, ranging from absenteeism to health care. These costs to American businesses soar into the billions (*The MetLife Study of Working Caregivers and Employer Health Care Costs*).

In a robust economy, those costs and challenges to employers can be absorbed or accommodated somewhat easier. But in the difficult times facing many of today's businesses, caregivers must function with extra care to avoid taxing the goodwill of employers and coworkers—as well as the "bottom line."

The caregiver who daily attends to the needs of the patient serves as a critical component of that patient's overall health. Although it's difficult to quantify the exact value added by a caregiver, all can agree that a gainfully employed caregiver is in the best interest of the patient.

Paychecks, housing, insurance, food—the entire patient-care ecosystem for many individuals—depends upon the physical, emotional, and professional health of the caregiver. Certainly not all patients have a family member or friend serving as a caregiver, and clearly not all caregivers maintain full-time employment. Yet, according to the studies, millions of American workers are serving as volunteer caregivers for an aging, disabled, or chronically ill loved one.

As someone who has faced this issue on an extreme level, I receive many requests to address this topic. My passion is to equip caregivers with easy and practical tips, not only for staying employed but also for excelling in the workplace.

One of the most challenging issues I face as a caregiver for twenty-eight years is balancing work and my wife's chronic and pressing medical issues.

I recall days that began normally. But on those "normal" days, my wife had been admitted to the hospital and scheduled for surgery by the time our sons' school let out. Juggling the medical crisis alone is challenging. Living up to work responsibilities, however, while somehow keeping the plates spinning—picking up children, fixing meals, and swinging by the hospital to meet with doctors—can make for extremely stressful workdays.

When the caregiver is the business owner or boss, scheduling work may be easier, but the stress of keeping the business going brings additional challenges.

Employees serving as caregivers regularly find themselves in tight work situations that often require appeasing one demand, while disappointing another. Saying "no" to a hurting family member in order to maintain work responsibilities can significantly strain an already-stretched home life. Saying "no" to an employer, however, presents a new basket of problems. Caregivers often find themselves balancing on a professional tightrope: not abusing the generosity of fellow employees and supervisors while keeping crises on the home front at bay.

Is it any wonder that many caregivers decline promotions—and the increased wages that accompany the increased responsibilities—in order to avoid the extra duties that comes with workplace advancement? Sometimes, it is even easier to leave the workforce altogether. The caregiver's decision to retreat from the workplace has permanent effects that ripple through the family, the community, and, when multiplied many times over, the nation's economy.

For many years, I took jobs I really did not aspire to, all for insurance and flexibility of schedule. Like many caregivers, my earning potential and advancement took hits on numerous occasions. Also, like many caregivers, I learned to adapt and "figured out how to make it work." Along the journey, I discovered that although many bosses and supervisors possessed understanding, they still required good communication about the circumstances.

It was while balancing work and caregiving that I learned the three "F's."

- Be FORTHRIGHT with the boss
- Ask for FLEXIBILITY
- Give a FAIR day's work

If you're a caregiver who's juggling responsibilities at work and at home, nobody needs to tell you how tough that job can be. But from personal experience, I can tell you that, while the job is hard, it's not impossible. You can be *both* a primary caregiver *and* a valuable addition to your workplace.

It is always your next move.

Napoleon Hill

———⟶•⟵———

Nothing is so exhausting as indecision,
and nothing is so futile.

Bertrand Russell

———⟶•⟵———

I made up my mind, but I made it up both ways.

Casey Stengel

Chapter 38

UNILATERAL DECISIONS

The best decision-makers are those who are
willing to suffer the most over their decisions
but still retain their ability to be decisive.

M. Scott Peck

Sitting across the table from a man caring for his wife who suffers from Parkinson's disease, I couldn't help but see the weariness in his eyes and on his face.

When a mutual friend asked me to meet with him, the comment was simply, "He's worn out, and I think you could be of help to him."

"Worn out" seemed to be an understatement.

Stirring his coffee, this retired physician reflected, "I miss playing golf with my friends."

Listening for a little while longer, I recalled what I have come to call the three "I's" that plague every caregiver:

- The loss of INDEPENDENCE
- The ISOLATION
- The loss of IDENTITY

Immediately identifying the first two, I asked him, "Do you have the resources to hire someone part-time?" The predictable response came quickly, "She's not comfortable with having someone come into our home." Noticing the avoidance of speaking in first-person singular, I simply replied, "I didn't ask what she was comfortable doing."

The loss of identity, where the wants and needs of a loved one consumes a caregiver, remains one of the most challenging components when it comes to helping a caregiver. From such phrases as, "We just got home from the hospital . . ." or "He's having a bad day . . ." or "Our days are filled with . . ."—speaking in first-person singular all but fades away.

I understand feeling that loss of identity—perhaps on levels few will. Serving as a caregiver since age twenty-two, I've never really known any other lifestyle as an adult. Daily teetering close to the edge of collapsing emotionally, physically, and/or financially wears on a soul, and it is a challenge facing 65 million Americans caring for loved ones.

Looking at this husband in torment, I gently but firmly stated, "You're not violating your marriage by making unilateral decisions." Adding, as he lifted his eyes, "Sometimes the ones we love can't see past their fear, their illness, or their pain. As caregivers, we have to think of the good of the 'unit' not just the sick/disabled person. That means we have to make decisions that will protect the health and well-being of the caregiver—even if it means going against the wants of the person receiving care."

A person in pain, on heavy medication, suffering from dementia, or dealing with a severe disability or illness can't always see beyond their immediate need. Their cries for relief often overpower the gentle whisper of wisdom that cautions us to take a break. The guilt of making unilateral decisions, particularly for spouses and children caring for elderly parents, can be crushing.

We're mobile, they're not.
They're in pain, we're not.
They cling—we feel suffocated.

These and other dynamics play out daily (often hourly) in the relationships of caregivers and their charges. In spite of the conflicting feelings, caregivers must get fresh air and allow themselves to step back and make hard decisions for the good of the patient and themselves—and they often have to do that while feeling horribly alone and scared.

Looking across the table at the coffee shop, I saw familiar feelings cascade over my new friend's face. A smart man, a capable man, a loving husband and father, and a weary and lonely caregiver—I knew his turmoil well, and my heart broke for him. Unlike someone who is warm and well-fed trying to relate to someone who is hungry and cold, we caregivers recognize and relate to each other because we live it.

I asked him point-blank, "How would you like to resume your Tuesday golf outings with your buddies, have lunch at the club, play another round in the afternoon—and then come home to find your wife bathed, dressed, the house clean, and dinner prepared?"

As the tears filled his eyes, he simply said, "I can't imagine how wonderful that would be."

"You are one phone call away from prying your hands off the wheelchair and putting them on the golf club—make the call."

To his credit, he phoned the service I recommended, and they worked a wonderful schedule of help coming to the house. His problem was not financial—it was guilt and conflicting emotions.

The best way to help a caregiver is to see and acknowledge the internal conflict those feelings create—and gently walk them through learning to make better choices to not only help themselves, but ultimately help those they are giving treasure, sweat, and even blood to help. The one we care for won't be helped by depleting ourselves emotionally, physically, and financially.

———————

A reporter once asked me, "WWJD (What would Jesus do) as a caregiver?"

I won't speculate on what Jesus would do; I can tell you what He did do: He delegated.

When Jesus saw his mother and the disciple whom he loved standing nearby, he said to his mother, "Woman, behold, your son!" Then he said to the disciple, "Behold, your mother!" And from that hour the disciple took her to his own home. John 19:26-27 ESV

If Jesus can delegate, it stands to reason that you can enlist help in order for you to take a breather.

For to be free is not merely to cast off one's chains,
but to live in a way that respects and
enhances the freedom of others.

Nelson Mandela

—⊷∘⊶—

Therefore don't worry about tomorrow,
because tomorrow will worry about itself.
Each day has enough trouble of its own.

Matthew 6:34 HCSB

Chapter 39

THEY'RE GOING TO FALL

A man's got to know his limitations.

Clint Eastwood as Dirty Harry

A woman once shared with me that she couldn't get away from her aging father because every time she left, something bad happened. "He falls each time I leave him with someone else!" she said, while tearing up in frustration.

"Something bad happens whether you are there or not," I told her. "You can't guarantee your presence will forever prohibit him from falling. If you've done your best to provide safeguards and to have someone there in the event of a fall or other mishaps, what more can you do?"

As we all struggle with the independence issue, these questions require consideration:

- Will your loved one's life improve if you are out of the picture?
- Are you able to care for them when you are emotionally and physically exhausted?
- Will they be better off once you're a "husk of a human being"?

Looking at those questions, "seeking and maintaining" a healthy level of emotional and even physical independence becomes critical not only for the caregiver but also for the patient as well. Independence is not abandonment; it's allowing a life to blossom on its own without encroachment.

I've watched my wife fall many times since she began walking on prosthetic limbs decades ago. Each time, I try to catch her if I can—and comfort her when I can't. The fact is: amputees who use prosthetic legs are going to fall. She's embarrassed when it happens, and I'm embarrassed for her. She hurts, and I hurt for her. Our sons hurt to see their mother fall. But we all recognize that for her to be who she is, she has to get back up and continue trying. That's her journey. If I, by the force of my will, tried to keep her in a wheelchair to avoid falling, I would do great harm to her—and ultimately to me. I would force her to become utterly dependent upon me and rob her of whatever level of independence she could achieve.

We're caregivers, not superheroes. We can't prevent every disaster or solve every problem. This isn't Metropolis; it's the real world. Here in the real world, they are going to fall. They will make mistakes. They will get hurt. No caregiver can eliminate those risks without endangering his or her well-being.

We do the best we can to protect the ones we love, while never forgetting that the best asset for *their* protection is to have a healthy caregiver.

Surrender to the Lord is not a tremendous sacrifice,
not an agonizing performance.
It is the most sensible thing you can do.

Corrie ten Boom

———◦◦◦———

I will lift up my eyes to the hills.
From whence comes my help?
My help comes from the LORD,
Who made heaven and earth.

Psalm 121:1–2 NKJV

———◦◦◦———

For what has been—thanks! For what shall be—yes!

Dag Hammarskjöld

Chapter 40

———— ❧ ————

THE SERENITY PRAYER

Stop quarreling with God!
If you agree with him, you will have peace at last,
and things will go well for you.

Job 22:21 NLT

The American theologian Reinhold Niebuhr composed a prayer containing one sentence that became known as the Serenity Prayer. Not limited to dealing with addiction issues, this prayer applies to every life situation—including our role as caregivers.

> "God, grant me the serenity
> to accept the things I cannot change,
> the courage to change the things I can,
> and the wisdom to know the difference."

Of course, Niebuhr's words are far easier to recite than they are to live by. But if my years as a caregiver have taught me anything, they've taught me to focus intently on the things I can change, to leave the rest up to God, and to accept His verdict *on everything*.

Everybody experiences adversity, but as caregivers, we're confronted with it every day. Some things we can control; many things we cannot.

Early in my caregiving journey, I tried to control everything. But eventually I learned that, unlike Clark Kent, I wasn't wearing Superman's cape underneath my navy blazer. There were some things I simply couldn't do. And there were some things I simply couldn't understand.

The ideal man bears the accidents of life with dignity and grace, making the best of circumstances.

Aristotle

For years, I've heard my father often share, "God's got this problem: He thinks HE's God."

When I made the decision to live out the underlying meaning of that statement, my life changed for the better. Recognizing that I am not responsible for results and other people's behaviors has imparted greater freedom to love and live without the burden of carrying something that isn't mine.

Although circumstances and challenges haven't changed, I am changing. I'm learning that I can respond without reacting. I can care for without carrying. I can be at peace in the midst of craziness.

My hope for you, as a caregiver and as a person, is that you come to terms with—and celebrate—yourself, your responsibilities, your loved ones, and your Creator. When you do, you can be comforted in the knowledge that your life as a caregiver is *both* a mission from above *and* a grand opportunity for service here below.

The first word in that prayer is "God." Just calling out is an act of faith and an admission of need. When it comes to seeking God's help, all we need is "need." We caregivers tend to push ourselves to inhuman levels before finally collapsing and admitting defeat. At that point, however, is when we can experience the grace, peace, and joy of God's presence and provision. That's the wisdom part of the prayer: realizing what we can and cannot do. We cannot change other people. We cannot change God.

We, however, can change. Our circumstances don't hold us in bondage. Those reality TV shows about cops often show criminals being arrested. Even though the bad guys struggle mightily at first, and cause all kinds of stress and pain to themselves and others, they all have one thing in common: They eventually stopped struggling. At some point their bodies simply run out of strength fighting against something bigger than themselves.

It's only a matter of time, however, before we simply give out from sheer exhaustion. We often look at a physical and/or emotional collapse as failure on our part. I say it is an opportunity for us to relinquish our faulty idea of control and step into a new life of faith and calmness.

It's at that point where we are invited to trust God for today, and ask for the strength to do what is in our power to do. We also humbly admit we are powerless and ask for the courage to accept our limits, and then ask for His wisdom to know what belongs to us and what doesn't.

That's why I borrowed the principles of "The Serenity Prayer" to write "The Caregiver's Prayer" at the beginning of this book. The first time that prayer is said, it will feel awkward, and maybe even pointless.

The 1,000th time, it won't.

TIPS FOR CAREGIVERS

1-2-30 Plan for Caregivers
H-E-L-P M-E Plan

Health

1 annual flu (or shingles) vaccination

2 well visits

30 minutes of daily exercises

Emotions

1 counseling session per month

2 support groups

30 days in church per year

Lifestyle

1 thing per week that YOU enjoy

2 weeks vacation from caregiving per year (may not be
possible in a "block")

30 minutes of laughter (daily—may not be possible in
a "block")

Profession

1 training class per year to learn a new skill

2 performance meetings with supervisor each year

30 minutes daily away from desk/phone

Money

> 1 charity you can financially support
>
> 2 meetings per year with a financial advisor
>
> $30 per paycheck into savings/investment

Endurance

> 1 daily contact with positive/loving friends or family members
>
> 2 hours per week of "Me time"
>
> 30 minutes daily devotional/quiet time.

For Weary Hearts

> 1 Savior
>
> 2 hymns *(Great Is Thy Faithfulness/It Is Well With My Soul)*
>
> 30 words: *Yea, though I walk through the valley of the shadow of death, I will fear no evil for thou art with me. Thy rod and Thy staff, they comfort me.*

ABOUT THE AUTHOR

A lifetime of experience. A lifeline for fellow caregivers.

Peter Rosenberger is president of Nashville-based *Standing With Hope,* an outreach whose flagship program provides artificial limbs to people in West Africa. Host of a weekly radio program, he's also an accomplished public speaker, writer, and spokesman for the needs of America's 65 million caregivers.

His is an unparalleled journey. As his wife's sole caregiver for nearly thirty years, he has labored through a medical nightmare that has mushroomed to 78 operations, the amputation of both her legs, and $9 million in medical bills. The experience and wisdom he has gleaned gives Peter a unique and astonishing understanding of health care issues facing millions of people. But more than that, he brings unmatched empathy for the deep heartache that causes even the strongest to falter.

"…One joke away from being a night club act," Peter combines deep compassion with a contagious humor to bring fresh air into the painful places faced by America's caregivers.

This is Rosenberger's third book.

To have Peter speak at your event or
to obtain additional books by Peter and Gracie,
visit www.standingwithhope.com

Peter Rosenberger's new app for caregivers is available on
the web and for iOS devices. View online at www.carekitapp.com
or search for **CareKit** in the AppStore.

Enter promo code "hope" for a free one-month trial.

GENETIC
DIVERSITY
AND
HUMAN
EQUALITY

GENETIC
DIVERSITY
AND
HUMAN
EQUALITY

Theodosius Dobzhansky

FOREWORD BY

Ward Madden

CHAIRMAN, COMMISSION ON LECTURES, THE JOHN DEWEY
SOCIETY FOR THE STUDY OF EDUCATION AND CULTURE

Basic Books, Inc., Publishers
NEW YORK

THE JOHN DEWEY SOCIETY LECTURE—NUMBER THIRTEEN

The John Dewey Lecture is delivered annually under the sponsorship of the John Dewey Society at the annual meeting of the National Society of College Teachers of Education. This book is an elaboration of the Lecture given on that occasion. The intention of the Series is to provide a setting where able thinkers from various sectors of our intellectual life can direct their most searching thought to problems that involve the relation of education to culture. Arrangements for the presentation and publication of the Lecture are under the direction of the John Dewey Society Commission on Lectures.

WARD MADDEN, *Brooklyn College, City University of New York, Chairman and Editor*

GEORGE E. AXTELLE
Southern Illinois University

VIRGIL CLIFT
New York University

ARNO A. BELLACK
Teachers College, Columbia University

GAIL KENNEDY
Amherst College

FOREWORD

H OW IS ONE to account for the fifteen or so points that separate the average scores of whites and blacks on conventional intelligence tests? And what is the meaning of the twenty-eight-point differential between the children of professional men and the children of unskilled workers? The standard answer of those with faith in the worth of the individual and the equality of men is that these differences are to be accounted for by environmental influences.

But some disturbing facts intrude. Why is it that identical twins reared together show an 87 percent correlation with one another in IQ, whereas unrelated children reared together show only a 24 percent correlation? Why do such twins, even when reared separately, still show a 75 percent correlation, whereas unrelated children reared separately show no correlation at all? Such studies seem to suggest that, even though the environment matters, its influence is heavily outweighed by genetic factors.

Various investigators, most recently Arthur R. Jensen in 1969, have concluded that intelligence is determined approximately 80 percent by heredity and only 20 percent by environment. This conclusion has encouraged the doubts existing in the minds of some that the children of the poor have the necessary genetic equipment to rise, in numbers proportional to their population, to higher positions in society. And it has supported, in some, doubts about the "inherent" ability of black Americans.

These questions are rarely discussed openly—but there is an insidious effect in the taboo itself. In the silence, the suspicion persists that not only may intelligence be more determined by genetics than by environment but also—what is especially disturbing—intelligence may be unequally distributed among the social classes and races.

Here and there, of late, there have been isolated calls that the whole question be reopened, and that a strong new effort be made in the objective spirit of science to ascertain and to understand in all its complexity the actual situation. It has been suggested that in the past the question has actually been neglected by serious researchers because of conscious and unconscious prohibitions in the collective and individual minds of scientists—generated by laudable but nevertheless misguided liberal-humanistic presuppositions.

Theodosius Dobzhansky agrees that more needs to be known. The subject should not—need not—be taboo, he says. And he shows us that a truly sophisticated analysis and interpretation of scientific evidence points toward conclusions quite different from those that currently seem to threaten the widely shared hope for a just and equal society.

Dr. Dobzhansky's work makes clear, as never before, that there is no conflict between our democratic social goals and the findings of science. We ned not fear the truth. Science has never inhibited men from realizing their ethical objectives, nor does it now. Only our own ignorance of the truth can frighten us into abandoning justice. Dr. Dobzhansky's brilliant little book lucidly explains where scientific research leaves off and where the realm of moral choice begins. It should be required reading for all Americans.

Ward Madden

PREFACE

J OHN DEWEY THOUGHT that philosophy should be more
than an academic vocation or a demonstration of intellectual
gymnastics: "There is probably no better way to realize
what philosophy is all about when it is living, not anti-
quarian, than to ask ourselves what criteria and what aims
and ideals should control our educational policies and undertakings." The same standard applies, I believe, to evolutionary biology. Although a biologist may do his research on
mice, Drosophila flies, plants, or bacteria, the ultimate aim
should be to contribute toward the understanding of man and
his place in the universe. Biology, and science as a whole,
should be anthropocentric, i.e., relevant to man. The "rele-
vance" goes deeper than technological, environmental, and
other so-called practical problems. Basic or fundamental
science is a humanistic enterprise. Dewey rightly regarded

separation of science from ethics and values "intellectual scandal." He was one of those who believed (in the words of Martin E. Malia) "that the life of the intellect yields not only scientific truth, but moral truth; that the moral truth is also inevitably social in nature; that there exists, therefore, in scientific and rational politics the aim of which is social justice, or equality; and that the men of intellect, by definition, are the chief bearers of this truth-which-is-justice." Cynics say that people use science merely to give a veneer of respectability to their selfish interests and bigotries. There is no denying that science is sometimes so used. Yet human conduct is also influenced by the beliefs that men hold, and science is increasingly important as a source of these beliefs. In particular, evolutionary biology is relevant to "aims and ideals" of "educational policies and undertakings."

The first two chapters of this book are parts of a single essay; a version of the first was given as the John Dewey Lecture on February 25, 1972, in Chicago, while a version of the second has been published in *Sexual Selection and the Descent of Man,* edited by Bernard G. Campbell (Aldine · Atherton, Inc., Chicago). The third chapter has been published in *Changing Perspectives on Man,* edited by Ben Rothblatt (University of Chicago Press). Thanks are due to the above publishers for permission to utilize these chapters in the present book. I wish also to express my gratitude to Professor Ward Madden and to the officers of the John Dewey Society for the honor of having been chosen a John Dewey Lecturer.

Theodosius Dobzhansky

CONTENTS

GENETIC
DIVERSITY
AND
HUMAN
EQUALITY

1

DIVERSITY OF INDIVIDUALS, EQUALITY OF PERSONS

Widespread in the modern world, though by no means universally accepted and practiced, is the doctrine that all men are or should be equals. Forcefully stated in the ringing sentences of the Declaration of Independence, it is familiar to every American. The idea of equality is an integral part of the American tradition, and also the source of what Myrdal (1962) called the American Dilemma. The idea frequently bogs down in confusion and apparent contradictions. Equality is confused with identity, and diversity with inequality. This confusion can be found even in the writings of some outstanding scientists who could have been expected to know better. Political propagandists, of both the extreme right and left, spread the confusion deliberately.

3

It would seem that the easiest way to discredit the idea of equality is to show that people are innately, genetically, and therefore irremediably diverse and unlike. The snare is, of course, that human equality pertains to the rights and to the sacredness of life of every human being, not to bodily or even mental characteristics. According to the 1952 UNESCO statement on race, "equality of opportunity and equality in law in no way depend, as ethical principles, upon the assertion that human beings are in fact equal in endowment."

Defenders of equality become entangled in the same snare when they attempt to minimize or deny human genetic diversity. They overlook, or fail to understand, that the diversity is an observable fact of nature, while equality is an ethical commandment. At least in principle, equality can be withheld from, or bestowed upon, members of a society or citizens of a state regardless of how similar or diverse they are. Inequality is also not biologically given but is rather a socially imposed prescription.

The Source of Genetic Diversity

Everyday experience shows that every person we meet is different from everybody met before. Even so-called identical, or monozygotic, twins are not really identical; they are recognizably separate persons. The recognition of individuality is a generalization derived from common practice, but the causes of individuality began to be understood only with the advent of biology, and particularly genetics. Mendel showed that parents heterozygous for the same n genes have the potentiality of producing 3^n genetically distinct kinds of progeny. Parents each of whom is heterozygous for n different genes are potentially capable of producing 4^n kinds of progeny. The question of the number of genes for which an average person is heterozygous has long been a matter of speculation and dispute. It now appears that the figure is at least in the thousands or ten thousands. Even though not all possible genetic endowments are equally probable, the genetic variety engendered in sexual reproduction is immense. Excepting only monozygotic twins and other monozygotic multiple births, the likelihood that any two persons alive, or having lived, or to live in the future, will be genetically identical is negligible. The source of the genetic variety is Mendelian recombination of genes in sexual reproduction; monozygotic multiple births result from asexual multiplication of sexually produced fertilized egg cells.

Human individuality manifests itself in all sorts of characteristics. Perhaps one of the most imposing examples is the rejection of skin grafts or organ transplants derived from other persons. Homografts, i.e., skin transplants from one part to another of the same person's body, are usually accepted without difficulty, as are transplants from one monozygotic twin to another. But a graft from another person, even a sibling, parent, or child, is usually rejected because of an immune reaction in the recipient. Only by rather drastic measures involving artificial suppression of antibody production in the recipient is it possible to have transplants derived from other persons, or even different species, temporarily adopted. For obvious reasons, these matters have been studied in greatest detail in experimental animals, namely mice. The studies have revealed numerous so-called histocompatibility genes; only if two individuals happen to carry the same forms (alleles) of these genes can allografts (transplants from one individual to another) be successful. Apart from monozygotic twins, such genetic similarity may occur among members of an inbred line, propagated for many generations by mating close relatives, usually brothers and sisters. Because of the universality of incest taboos in man, prolonged inbreeding of this sort is not found in human populations.

Genetic individuality in man and other sexually reproducing species is also demonstrable by examination of some biochemical characteristics. The existence of a variety of blood groups, recondite but important differences of the red blood cells which must be guarded against in blood transfusions, has been known since early in the current century. More recently, genetically determined variants of some enzymes (allozymes) have attracted attention. Studies on several species of Drosophila flies have shown that an average individual in natural populations is heterozygous for between 10 and 20 percent of the genes determining allozyme variants. A similar situation appears to prevail in human populations. It is not certain that the allozyme genes studied are a fair sample of all genes possessed by an organism. The number of genes in a human sex cell is also not known—recent estimates range from a hundred thousand to several million. However, taking the figures of 10 to 20 percent of heterozygous genes at face value, the number of potentially possible gene constellations turns out to be far greater than the number of subatomic particles estimated by physicists to exist in the whole universe. One inevitable conclusion is that only a minute fraction of possible genetic endowments can ever appear in the human or any other biological species.

Whether the genetic diversity of allozyme variants, or of

histocompatibility genes, is of much significance socially may, of course, be questioned. At first thought, the answer seems to be negative. With the exception of some pathological variants, one's form of enzyme or of blood groups seems to make no difference. However, genes may have so-called pleiotropic effects, and modify several characteristics. Thus, many hereditary diseases caused by changes in single genes are "syndromes" of seemingly quite unrelated characteristics. One cannot rule out the possibility that apparently neutral, neither useful nor harmful, genetic variants may have unsuspected concomitants in the physiological and mental sphere. For example, it has been claimed that the B, A, and O blood groups are related to resistance to plague, smallpox, and syphilis, respectively. The validity of this claim is still under scrutiny.

Genes and Environments

Genetic conditioning of many human traits that unquestionably matter to their possessors and to the societies in which they occur is established with varying degrees of certainty for different traits. The word "conditioning," instead of "determination," is here used advisedly. Intelligence, personality, special abilities, and other traits are susceptible to modification by genetic as well as environmental factors. What, then, is the meaning of the often-heard statement that the intelligence of a person is determined by his genes? It certainly does not mean that a possessor of these genes must necessarily have this and no other degree or kind of intelligence, because the same gene constellation could have resulted in either a higher or a lower intelligence in different circumstances. The genes have *determined* the intelligence (or stature or weight) of a person only in the particular sequence of environments to which that person has been exposed in his upbringing and life experiences. What actually develops is *conditioned* by the interplay of the genes with the environments. Every person is unique and nonrecurrent. No two individuals, except monozygotic twins, have the same genes; not even monozygotic twins have the same environment.

Now let us consider people in general rather than a particular person. What the genes really determine are the reaction ranges exhibited by individuals with more or less similar genes over the entire gamut of possible environments. The concept of reaction range is important, and is curiously difficult for some people to grasp. Heredity is not a status but a process. Genetic traits are not preformed in the sex cells, but emerge in the course of development, when potentialities determined by the genes are realized in the process of development in certain environments. Similar genes may have different effects in dissimilar environments, and so may dissimilar genes in similar environments.

Although it is often said that the genes determine the upper and the lower limits which a trait, such as intelligence or stature, can reach, this is not a useful formulation. Existing environments are endlessly variable, and new ones are constantly added. To test the reactions of a given gene constellation (or a cluster of kindred ones) in all environments is obviously impossible. For example, how could one discover the highest stature that I could have reached in some very propitious environment, or the lowest one at which I could have stopped growing and still remained alive? It is even more farfetched to forecast the stature in environments that may be engineered in the future, perhaps with the aid of some new growth hormone.

The idea that intelligence and other socially significant human traits may be hereditary is repugnant to many people, largely because of confusion of heredity with fate or predestination. A genetic conditioning of the variations in intelligence does not necessarily mean that the intelligence of a person is irremediably fixed by his genes. It can be enhanced or stunted by upbringing, training, and disease. In principle, any trait is subject to modification by genetic as well as environmental means. The more that is known about the developmental physiology of a trait, the greater is the feasibility of influencing it in directions that are regarded as desirable.

Suppose, for the sake of argument, that the average intelligence of representatives of some class or race is higher or lower than the averages for other classes or races in the environments that exist at present in our society. Would this justify race and class prejudice? Not at all, because even with our present pitifully inadequate knowledge, important changes in manifested intelligence can be induced by intensive care and tutoring of children (Heber, 1968). With altered rearing and educational environments, the disparity of group averages may conceivably be nullified or reversed. One often hears that those who give credence to developmental flexibility of human traits fear that studies on class and race averages might disclose the dreadful fact that these averages are genetically conditioned. Such fears can be experienced only by those who misunderstand the nature of genetic conditioning.

We need to ascertain the reaction repertories of the available variety of human genetic endowments in existing and feasible physical, nutritional, educational, and social environments. The importance of research in this field can hardly be overestimated. Yet the knowledge of which environments are most propitious for realization of socially desirable potentialities of human genetic endowments remains inadequate, despite some spectacular achievements of educational and medical research. Agricultural research is in principle a similar endeavor applied to domesticated animals and cultivated plants. But an agriculturist can at present go further than a sociologist, and can intervene to modify the genetic constitutions of the animals and plants concerned. The modification is directed toward making them develop in the environments in which they are placed in ways most advantageous to man. Analogous intervention in man's development is envisaged by various eugenical programs, but this is a task largely for the future. In any case, genetic conditioning, no matter how strong, does not preclude improvement by manipulation of the environments.

Genetic and Environmental Conditioning of IQ

By far the most abundant information on the distribution and genetics of any mental trait in man is that on the intelligence quotient (IQ). There is nevertheless much uncertainty, and inconclusive polemics, as to the precise nature of the "intelligence" that the IQ measures. I do not intend to masquerade as a psychologist, and for orientation in the problems in this field must refer the reader to the works of Anastasi (1958), Brown (1965), Butcher (1968), Thomson (1967), Tyler (1965), and references therein. My excuse for intruding on this domain is that recent sensational and inflammatory pronouncements about the genetics of IQ differences between socioeconomic classes and races have attracted public attention. A critical consideration of the genetic aspects of the situation is in order.

No competent scientist takes the IQ as a measure of overall quality or worth of human beings (although a part of the public has been misled into believing this). The possessor of a high IQ may be vicious, selfish, lazy, and slovenly, and a lower IQ may be combined with kindness, altruism, and hard and careful work. Burt (1961) is one of those who claim that "we may say , assert that the innate amount of potential ability with which a child is endowed at birth sets an upper limit to what he can possibly achieve at school or in afterlife," and that IQ measures this supposedly innate ability. Others deny that IQ testing provides any scientifically valid information, and see in it merely a device used by the privileged classes to maintain their status at the expense of the underprivileged ones. It is unfortunate that the writings of Jensen (1969), Eysenck (1971), and some others are eagerly exploited by racist propagandists, perhaps without consent of the scientific investigators themselves.

The extravagant claims and counterclaims should not preclude a rational view of the issue. The warrant for IQ testing is simply its statistical predictive power. Even though just what mental and psychophysiological traits are included in the IQ scores is not conclusively established, it is undeniable that there are significant statistical correlations among IQ scores, success in schooling, advancement in the occupational structure as at present organized, and, at some removes, prestige and pecuniary rewards meted out in western capitalist or "postindustrial" societies. It is important to keep in mind that, since the correlations are not perfect, the IQ does not forecast reliably the achievement of an individual tested. The predictive power may also be limited in societies structured very differently from ours, such as Chairman Mao's China or that of the Kalahari Bushmen.

That differences between individuals in whatever qualities the IQ tests measure are genetically as well as environmentally conditioned is now securely established. Since the IQ is correlated with scholastic achievement, the latter is also, though to a lesser extent, genetically and environmentally conditioned. Evidence of genetic conditioning is ample; it comes from more than 50 independent studies in 8 different countries, and comprises more than 30,000 correlational pairings. It has been carefully and critically summarized in a brief article by Erlenmeyer-Kimling and Jarvik (1963), and in more detailed form by Jensen (1969). Median correlation coefficients obtained are shown in Table 1–1.

In the human species more than in any other, relatives "inherit" similar genes as well as similar environments. Therefore, a close resemblance of monozygotic twins to each other would not by itself demonstrate that IQ is under genetic control. However, the fact that the resemblance of monozygotics is appreciably greater than the resemblance among dizygotics makes this irrefutable. To be sure, the objection has been raised that since parents, playmates, teachers, and so on, treat monozygotic twins more alike than they do dizygotic ones, the environments of the former are more similar than those of the latter. But this is a misapprehension.

TABLE 1-1

Median correlation coefficients between IQs of persons of different degrees of relationship (after Spuhler and Lindzey, 1967; and Jensen, 1969).

Relationship	Number of of Studies	Median Correlation
Twins, monozygotic, reared together	14	+0.87
Twins, monozygotic, reared apart	4	+0.75
Twins, dizygotic, same sex	11	+0.56
Twins, dizygotic, different sex	9	+0.49
Siblings, reared together	36	+0.55
Siblings, reared apart	33	+0.47
Parent and child	13	+0.50
Grandparent and grandchild	3	+0.27
First cousins	3	+0.26
Unrelated children, reared together	5	+0.24
Unrelated children, reared apart	4	−0.01
Foster parent and child	3	+0.20

Parents and other people rarely know for sure whether a given pair of twins are mono- or dizygotic. The greater similarity of the environments of monozygotic twins is a consequence of their genetic similarity. Genetics and environment in man are covariant.

The IQs of monozygotic twins reared together are correlated more strongly than they are in those reared apart. This is obviously a matter of environment. Yet the monozygotics reared apart remain more similar on the average than dizygotics reared together. This is a matter of genetics. The correlations observed between dizygotic twins, siblings, and children reared by their parents fall between + 0.47 and + 0.56. Since all these categories of relatives share on the average the same proportions of genes, 50 percent, we have further evidence of geñʊʲʲ conditioning. Grandparents and grandchildren have on the aveʲoɣe 25 percent of the genes in common, and the intercorrelatioɫʲ between them are correspondingly reduced. Most impressive eviʲʊʲʲʲe, despite some possible biases in the data, comes from testʲʊʲ adopted children along with their adoptive or foster parents and their biological parents. Adopted children evidently have genes in common with the biological, but share the environments with the adoptive parents. However, their IQs correlate more closely with the biological than with the adoptive parents. Siblings reared together are more similar than unrelated children reared together, just as the latter are more similar than unrelated children reared apart.

It is important to realize the meaning as well as the limitations of the above evidence. Almost all of it comes from studies on Caucasian and predominantly middle-class people (an exception is Vandenberg, 1970, who studied some black twins). Neither the twins, nor siblings reared apart, nor adopted children, have been exposed to the full range of environments which occur in the societies in which they live, not to speak of mankind as a whole. It can be seen in Table 1–1 that the IQs of monozygotic twins reared apart remain considerably more similar than those of dizygotic twins, and siblings reared apart are more similar than unrelated children reared together. How far the observed correlations could be lowered by greater environmental heterogeneity remains an open problem, although no conceivable heterogeneity is likely to reduce it to zero.

The work of Heber (1968) has already been mentioned. It describes an experiment on ghetto children whose mothers had IQs below 70. Some of these children received special care and training, while others were a control group. Four years after the training period the IQs of the former averaged 127 and those of the latter 90, a spectacular difference of 37 points. The fact that the control children had a 20-point advantage over their mothers is not unexpected. The IQs of their fathers are unknown, but may have been considerably above those of the mothers. Furthermore, such an advantage could come from the well-known genetic phenomenon of regression toward the mean: the progeny of parents above the population mean do not on the average attain the parental values, while those with parents below the population mean generally exceed the parental values. Regression toward the mean is observed with all sorts of traits, such as stature and body proportions, and it is only natural to find it with IQs.

The work of Skodak and Skeels (1949) is equally impressive. They studied the correlations between the IQs of adopted children and those of their biological and adoptive mothers, finding the latter correlations lower than the former. This does not mean that the IQ values of these children were like those of their biological parents. They were substantially higher (106 in children, 85.5 in their mothers), although not attaining the average levels of the adoptive parents or the biological offspring of the latter. This yields a simple conclusion: the genetic conditioning of IQs does not make them impervious to environmental modification.

The Heritability Controversy

Human stature varies from giant to dwarf and includes everything in between. In each population a certain mean or average stature is most frequent, small deviations from the mean are common, and large deviations are rare. Variance is a measure of the variability in a given population. It is computed as a sum of squared deviations from the mean, divided by the number of observations. The variance is evidently a compound of genetic and environmental variability; people may be predisposed by their genes to grow tall or short, but the growth may be stimulated or stunted by a variety of environmental factors. Several approaches have been used to measure which portions of the variance are attributable to genetic causes and which to environmental ones. Heritability is a statistic computed as a ratio (or percentage) of the genetic to total observed variance. Heritability "in the broad sense" and "in the narrow sense" may be distinguished, but this is a fairly recondite matter which need not detain us here. The latter heritability is particularly useful for prediction of the gains to be expected from selection practiced by breeders of domestic animals and plants, for example, selection to increase the number of eggs laid by hens or yield of milk from cows. With man such predictions are not yet practicable, because natural selection is hard to measure and artificial selection is a concern for the future.

The heritability of IQ in man is estimated from data of the sort summarized in Table 1–1. Slightly different estimates are obtained from different varieties of IQ tests, from correlations between relatives of various degrees, and between relatives of the same degree reared together and apart. The available estimates have been carefully reviewed by Thomson (1967), and especially by Jensen (1969). Jensen gives an overall estimate of 0.81 (81 percent). This is a high heritability, as the list of heritabilities of various traits in different organisms, compiled in Table 1–2, clearly shows. IQ is about as strongly heritable as human stature. Its heritability is much higher than those of egg production in poultry or of yield in corn. Yet the selection practiced on these latter traits by animal and plant breeders has resulted in substantial improvements. Behavior traits in Drosophila, responses to light and to gravity, have heritabilities an order of magnitude lower than IQ. Genetic conditioning of human characters as little heritable as these would probably be undetectable, and yet artificial selection for some ten to twenty generations induces spectacular changes in the behavior of Drosophila flies.

There has been so much misunderstanding of the significance of the high heritability of IQ that it is imperative to make clear what this heritability does and does not mean. To begin with, it does not mean that the IQ, or scholastic achievement insofar as the latter is a product of IQ, is not subject to modification by upbringing and other environmental means. The cited works of Heber, Skodak, and Skeels have shown this clearly. Even more basic is that the heritability is not an intrinsic property of a trait but of the population in which it occurs. Consideration of limiting cases makes this obvious. Suppose we have a population consisting of genetically identical individuals; all traits would then have zero heritability. A bit less unrealistic is to envisage a population in which all members live in identical environments; all heritabilities would then be equal to unity. Therefore, estimates of heritability are valid only for the populations and for the times when the data on which they are based were collected.

The dependence of heritability on the degree of genetic

TABLE 1–2

*Examples of heritability estimates in various animals
and plants.*

Organism and Trait	Heritability
Spotting in Friesian cattle	0.95
Slaughter weight in cattle	0.85
Stature in man	0.81
IQ in man	0.81
Weight in man	0.78
Cephalic index in man	0.75
Plant height in corn	0.70
Egg weight in poultry	0.60
Weight of fleece in sheep	0.40
Milk production in cattle	0.30
Yield in corn	0.25
Egg production in poultry	0.20
Egg production in Drosophila	0.20
Ear length in corn	0.17
Litter size in mice	0.15
Response to light in Drosophila	0.09
Conception rate in cattle	0.05
Response to gravity in Drosophila	0.04

and environmental uniformity or heterogeneity must be kept
in mind in evaluations of the significance of differences observed in IQ and other human traits. With the exception to
be mentioned below, the information on which the heritability estimates for IQ are based comes from studies on white
and predominantly middle-class populations. Most abundant
data pertain to monozygotic and dizygotic twins and siblings
reared together, i.e., in the same families. The environments
in which children are brought up in the same family are
certainly not identical, but they are also not as divergent as
they are in families that belong to different socioeconomic
classes, castes, or races in different parts of the world. Ex-

amples of twins and siblings being reared apart are understandably infrequent, and when they are found they are likely to be placed in not too dissimilar environments.

IQ Differences in Social Classes

If the estimation of the heritability of IQ differences between individual members of the same population is beset with pitfalls, the complexities increase greatly when differences between population means are considered. Since educational and other opportunities are often very unequal for children of different socioeconomic classes, it is not unexpected that their mean IQs and scholastic achievements are also unequal. Burt (1961), Eckland (1967, 1972a, b), and Gottesman (1968a, b) have critically reviewed the pertinent evidence. A short summary of Burt's data on some 40,000 adults and their children in England appears in Table 1–3. Higher professional (I), lower professional (II), clerical (III), skilled (IV), semiskilled (V), and unskilled (VI) occupations are distinguished. The average IQs of the fathers in these categories vary from 139.7 for the higher professionals to 84.6 for unskilled workers. However, the children of the high-scoring fathers are on the average below, and of low-scoring fathers above, the parental means. This is the phenomenon of regression toward the mean well known to geneticists, and already mentioned. Regardless of whether the IQ differences between occupational classes are mainly genetic or mainly environmental, it is clear that the children do not fully inherit either the superior or the inferior performance of their parents.

The situation is analogous with human races. People who

TABLE 1–3

Average IQs of fathers and of their children belonging to socioeconomic classes from I, the highest, to VI, the lowest (after Burt, 1961).

	I	II	III	IV	V	VI
IQs of fathers	139.7	130.6	115.9	108.2	97.8	84.6
IQs of children	120.8	114.7	107.8	104.6	98.9	92.6
Frequency per 1,000	3	31	122	258	325	261

belong to different races, when they live in different countries as well as when they live side by side in the same territory, do not always have equal opportunities for either bodily or mental development. But while members of socioeconomic classes are not as a rule recognizable by physical traits, races usually have externally visible "stigmata" which lead to self-identification and to identification by others. Endless disputes and passionate polemics arise from the finding that the white and black populations in the United States also differ in IQ averages. Assuredly, individual scores are broadly overlapping; many whites score below the black mean, and many blacks are above the white mean. However, the black average is some 15 IQ points below the white average.

Class and race differences in IQ averages may be ascribed to inequalities in educational opportunities and living standards. This explanation is traditionally favored by most social scientists and by political liberals. On the other hand, the differences may be genetic, which is pleasing to racists and reactionaries, but not espoused by any reputable scientist. Finally, both environmental and genetic conditionings may be involved. The bone of contention is then not environment versus heredity, but how much environmental relative to genetic conditioning.

The controversy is growing hotter because of the finding that individual IQ differences have large genetic components. Racists try to obtain maximum propaganda mileage from this fact. Yet the differences between race and class averages need not be genetically conditioned to the same degree as individual differences. Nobody, not even racists, can deny that living conditions and educational opportunities are disparate in races and classes. Jensen (1969), after recognizing explicitly that the heritability of individual differences within a population cannot validly be used as a measure of the heritability of the population means, tries to do just that. In fairness to him, it must be conceded that he presents a most detailed analysis of the environmental factors which could be instrumental in bringing about the divergence of IQ averages in the white and black populations of the United States. His conclusion is that none of the factors, or combinations of factors, give an adequate explanation of this divergence, which accordingly must be largely genetic. I remain unconvinced by his argumentation.

Scarr-Salapatek (1971a, b) may have achieved a breakthrough in heritability studies. The assumption made heretofore in IQ analyses has been that the action of genetic and environmental factors is simply additive. In other words, genetic and environmental agencies that bring about increments and decrements of intelligence (and other mental traits) act independently of one another, and always in the same way. This need not be so at all. Genetic differences may manifest themselves conspicuously in people who develop in favorable and stimulating environments, and remain undisclosed in adverse or suppressive environments. Carriers of genetic endowments who could unfold high IQs under favorable conditions will fare no better than genetically less well endowed people in suppressive environments. If this is so, the heritability of IQ should be lower among disadvantaged socioeconomic groups (classes as well as races) than among the privileged ones. On the other hand, the heritabilities should be uniform if the simple additivity hypothesis is valid. The two hypotheses are empirically testable, and Scarr-Salapatek has made an ingenious and discerning effort to test them.

Among 250,258 children in Philadelphia schools, from kindergarten to the twelfth grade, 3,042 twin pairs were found; 36 percent of the twins were white and 64 percent black. Regrettably, tests could not be made to identify the monozygotic and the dizygotic pairs (presumably because of the expense involved). Obviating this handicap involved resorting to a rather complex statistical operation. Among the twins, 1,028 pairs were of the same sex and 493 were of opposite sexes. These latter were dizygotic. Among the same-sexed twins, there must also have been approximately 493 dizygotics, with the rest monozygotic. This group was, accordingly, a mixture of not individually identifiable mono- and dizygotic twins. The families of the twins were classified according to their socioeconomic status: above median, median, and below median. As expected, the black families were more often disadvantaged:

	Below	Median	Above
Black	634	236	134
White	114	106	340

Aptitude and scholastic achievement test scores of the twins were analyzed statistically. On aptitude tests (where the national mean is 50) the following socioeconomic class and race averages were found:

	Below	Median	Above
Black	27.7	29.7	33.0
White	34.8	43.4	50.9

Differences between the upper- and the lower-class children among the blacks are much smaller (5.3) than among the whites (16.1). What is more important is that the variance of the test scores is greater in the advantaged than in the disadvantaged groups, among both blacks and whites. A greater proportion of the variances found in the relatively privileged than in the underprivileged socioeconomic classes is attributable to genetic causes. This is what the hypothesis of interaction between the genetic and environmental factors (see above) has predicted. The conclusion of Scarr-Salapatek is worth quoting:

From studies of middle-class white populations, investigators have reached the conclusion that genetic variability accounts for about 75 percent of the total variance in IQ scores of whites. A closer look at children reared under different conditions shows that the percentage of genetic variance and the mean scores are very much a function of the rearing conditions of the population. A first look at the black population suggests that genetic variability is important in advantaged groups, but much less important in the disadvantaged. Since most blacks are socially disadvantaged, the proportion of genetic variance in the aptitude scores of black children is considerably less than that of the white children, as predicted by model 1 [environmental determination].

Evolutionary Genetics of Caste and Class

The question is sometimes asked: How do you define "man"? Biologically the answer is simple. All human beings are members of a single species, *Homo sapiens*. Though some pathological variants seem to be less than human, they belong to our species. Their genes come from the same gene pool as everybody else's. Inhabitants of the whole world share in the common gene pool of the species. Perhaps no hybrids of Eskimos and Tungus with Hottentots and Aboriginal Australians have ever been produced, but there are unbroken chains of intercrossing of geographically intermediate populations. Assuredly, this does not mean that mankind is a single uniform breeding population, wherein every individual would have equal chance to mate with any individual of the opposite sex anywhere. The population of our species is complexly subdivided into a variety of subordinate Mendelian breeding populations. In each of these, the probability of marriage within is greater than between populations.

Geographic, national, linguistic, religious, economic, and other factors keep the gene pools of the subordinate breeding populations partly, but probably never entirely, separate. Mendelian breeding populations within a species are more often than not overlapping, which does not make them unreal. The population of New York City has WASPs, Jews, Catholics, and blacks; wealthy, moderately well-off, poor, and destitute; educated and ignorant; people of English, Irish, Italian, Greek, and other ethnic groups, partly preserving their cultural backgrounds. Many individuals belong at the same time to two or more of these subpopulations or "isolates."

All these subdivisions are not only social and economic but also biological—a fact which may not be pleasing to social scientists who would like to make their field entirely autonomous from biology. But in man sociological and biological factors are almost always intertwined. The social subdivisions have biological consequences because they influence the choice of marriage partners. Marriages within each subpopulation are more frequent than are intermarriages. The subordinate Mendelian populations may become and may be maintained genetically distinct. The distinctions are almost always quantitative rather than qualitative. That is, gene variants which control some traits, from blood groups to intelligence, may be species-wide in distribution, and yet be found more frequently in some subpopulations than in others. This is not a biological technicality but a fact of cardinal ethical and political importance. Every person must be rated according to his individual qualities, regardless of the subpopulation from which his genes came.

All human societies, even the allegedly "classless" ones (e.g., the Soviet-type communist societies), are stratified into classes. People of a class have life chances in common, as determined by their power to dispose of goods and skills for the sake of income (Lipset, 1968). Classes are not only socioeconomic groups but also breeding populations, to a greater or lesser extent separate from other populations. It is therefore legitimate to ask whether their gene pools are different, and, if so, to what extent (Eckland, 1967; Gottesman, 1968b). The question can be inverted: To what extent, if at all, is the socioeconomic level a function of the genetic constitution?

Members of privileged classes like to believe that everybody belongs to the socioeconomic class for which his genes qualify him. The poor live wretchedly; if this is not through their faults, then it is owing to their genetic inferiority. The opulent and the mighty deserve their affluence because their genes entitle them to it. Such views are an abomination, not to the underprivileged alone but to some prosperous liberals as well. In their protest they often go out on a limb, espousing the indefensibly extremist position that the genetic basis of mankind is uniform everywhere, and need not be considered further. The article of Fried (1968) is a specimen of this genre, written by an anthropologist. The problem can, however, be approached in a less emotionally charged way.

Both as social groups and as breeding populations, socioeconomic classes vary in the degree of their separateness. Caste societies are at one pole and open-class societies at the other. Castes existed, and to some extent continue to exist, not only in India but in many traditional societies, including feudal and capitalist Europe, and to a lesser extent the United States. One belongs to the caste in which one is born, and marries somebody in the same caste. Castes occupy superior or inferior ranks in self-esteem and in the opinion of others. A "society" matron places herself unhesitatingly above the "rabble," which thus becomes another and more numerous caste. The matron is aghast at the thought that her daughter or son may marry someone not of "society," but is a little more indulgent of extramarital affairs and even of illegitimate progeny. The latter are not unimportant genetically. No caste, not even in traditional India, was genetically completely segregated.

Open-class societies permit, or even encourage, social mobility from class to class. People move into, or are coopted by, classes for which they are eligible according to their abilities and achievements. This is the principle of meritocracy. The class is determined not by birth but by personal qualities. The existing societies also form a spectrum in this respect, extending from at least theoretically impervious castes, through more or less rigidly closed, to progressively more meritocratic open classes. Various degrees of closure may be found in the same society. The blacks in the United States can, for the purposes of the present discussion, be treated as a caste rather than a race. Gene exchange between the black and the white castes was, until recently, mainly in one direction, from white to black, and that by way of extramarital unions. The black as well as the white castes contain a variety of socioeconomic classes between which social mobility and gene exchange are regarded acceptable.

We have seen that individual variability within classes and castes is both genetically and environmentally conditioned. This is true of IQ as well as of scholastic aptitude and achievement. The genetic component seems to be more pronounced in relatively more prosperous than among underprivileged socioeconomic groups. It should be kept in mind that IQ is not a unitary trait determined by a single gene; it is a composite of numerous genetic components. The IQ is surely not alone in being genetically conditioned. Less detailed but still substantial evidence suggests that many personality characteristics and special abilities, from mathematics to music, have genetic components in their variability.

It is not an overstatement to say that whenever a variable human trait, down to such far-fetched ones as smoking habits, has been studied genetically, indications of some genetic conditioning have come to light.

It is utterly unlikely that, in meritocratic societies, the incidence of all genetically conditioned behavior traits could remain uniform throughout the whole gamut of socioeconomic classes. A gloss is needed here to ward off a frequent misconception. The statement that genes for such traits as higher or lower IQs, keen eyesight, or musicianship are more common in a class or caste A than in B does not mean that all A persons and no B individuals possess these genes. Let me reiterate that, since not all-or-none but only gene frequency differences are involved, an individual's potentialities are determined by his own genetic endowment and not by his class or race origins.

In western societies the trend for several centuries has been from closed caste-like to open meritocratic societies. When western civilization achieved world-wide influence, the trend became universal. Social mobility is increasingly free. In a meritocracy, scholastic ability and achievement are among the paramount determiners of social mobility. Schools and universities are principal ladders for socioeconomic rise. Insofar as achievement is genetically conditioned, social mobility is a genetic as well as socioeconomic process. In Eckland's (1967) words: ". . . talented adults rise to the top of the social hierarchy and the dull fall or remain on the bottom. Therefore, as the system strives to achieve full equality of opportunity, the observed within-class variance among children tends to diminish while the between-class variance tends to increase on the selective traits associated with genetic differences."

Equality of opportunity is an ideal approached in various degrees, but not fully achieved anywhere. This enhances the importance of the argument that, while socioeconomic classes may and probably do differ in statistical averages of some traits, the differences between individual members far exceed the differences between class averages. To quote Eckland again:

. . . genetic variability guarantees a relatively substantial pool of very bright children from lower-class backgrounds, which is sufficient reason, in both utilitarian and ideological terms, for social policies that emphasize the importance of this overlap. Moreover, when entire groups of children from these backgrounds are systematically deprived of some opportunities for development . . . then the size of this pool is larger than that which otherwise might be estimated on the basis of heritability coefficients alone.

It may chagrin some people to learn that increasing equality of opportunity enhances, not reduces, genetic differences between socioeconomic classes. We shall see, however, that if the equality were made perfect, or nearly so, the classes as we know them now would no longer exist.

Wisdom of Equality and Unwisdom of Inequality

Human equality is an ethical precept, not a biological phenomenon. A society can grant or withhold it from its members. Whether or not ethics are deducible from scientific knowledge need not concern us here, but it is legitimate, and even necessary, to scrutinize the probable consequences of adoption or rejection of a given ethic. There were, and still exist, blatant inequalities in some societies, and various approaches to equality in others. Contrasts of this sort may be found simultaneously in the same society: caste-like segregation and denial of equality to the blacks coexisted until recently in the United States with a relative unconstraint of social mobility among the whites.

One may distinguish equality of opportunity and equality of status. "Whereas equality of status deals with how power, privilege, and prestige are distributed in a society, equality of opportunity deals with the process of status allocation or, in other words, the criteria by which people are selected to fill different roles in society" (Eckland, 1972). Even though equalizations of opportunity and of status usually go hand in hand, they may also diverge. Russia is a prime example of this. The revolution there has enhanced equality of opportunity (without making it anywhere near complete); status inequalities in U.S.S.R. became, if anything, magnified by the totalitarian bureaucratic regime.

A caste system entails inequalities of status as well as of opportunity. It also entails occupational specialization. Each of the numerous castes and subcastes in classical India had a business, trade, or work traditionally reserved to it. The problems of training and allocation of status were thus simplified—everybody knew from childhood what the source of his livelihood would be, and in what kind of occupation or toil he must become skilled. Of course, one belonged to the caste of one's parents, and had to marry a person of the same caste. One could not be promoted or demoted to another caste, no matter what one's achievements, failures, talents, or incapacities. Upper-caste status automatically carried with it respect and privilege; lower castes and outcastes ("untouchables") were subjected to gross indignities.

The system was revoltingly unjust from our modern point of view, yet it had a plausible-sounding rationale. Bose (1951), no partisan of the caste system, wrote: "The careful way in which the tradition of close correspondence between caste and occupation was built up is clear indication of what the leaders of Hindu society had in mind. They believed in the hereditary transmissibility of character, and thought it best to fix a man's occupation, as well as his status in life, by means of the family in which he had been born." The same rationale is offered by racists in the United States and elsewhere for the denial of equality to the black caste. Here is a specimen of Putnam's (1967) specious reasoning: "The relationship as to both employment and welfare which existed for generations between white and Negro families in the South was almost ideal because it was based upon reality. The white family took a cradle-to-grave responsibility for the Negro family and the latter repaid the former in faithful service." This idyllic (to Putnam and his like) relationship assumed that the blacks are genetically specialized for work in no capacity other than as domestic servants. The fatal flaw of all caste systems is that they are built explicitly or implicitly on such assumptions.

The caste system in India was the grandest genetic experiment ever performed on man. The structure of the society endeavored for more than two millennia to induce what we would now call genetic specialization of the caste populations for performance of different kinds of work and functions. Such specialization has not been achieved. The evidence is as yet insufficient to rule out the possibility that some average differences between the caste populations may exist. This much is certain: although modern India has far to go to abolish inequalities of status and opportunity, all castes have produced persons of ample competence to acquire nontraditional education and to engage in nontraditional occupations. Less far-ranging genetic experiments were revolutionary overturns of old elites, which were physically annihilated or forced to emigrate to other countries. Predictions were freely made that such intellectual decapitations would lead to a dearth of talent and competence. The test case of Russia has proved the prediction wrong; talent recruited from the former lower classes, which had no opportunity to manifest itself, has given rise to a new intelligentsia in no way inferior to the old one. An even more drastic test in China awaits completion.

The failures of caste systems are understandable in the light of genetics. Human populations, like those of most sexual and outbreeding species, have enormous stores of all kinds of genetic variability. Even with artificial selection directed specifically to this end, it is practically impossible to obtain a population completely homozygous for all its genes. Close inbreeding, such as brother-sister mating for many generations, is more likely to result in genetic uniformity, but it is hard to control just what genetic endowment will become fixed. Anyway, neither strong artificial selection nor close inbreeding have ever been systematically practiced in the human species, and there is no immediate prospect of their adoption. Ours, happily, is not Huxley's *Brave New World*. All human populations, even the relatively inbred ones, conserve ample supplies of genetic variance.

The gene pool of every caste generates genetic endowments whose carriers could perform competently, and even achieve excellence, in occupations reserved by custom for other castes. For the sake of argument, assume that a caste population was at some point in time genetically better adapted than other castes for some task. There existed castes of priests, scholars, warriors, tradesmen, and so on. Could the differential adaptedness be maintained for many generations, except by systematic training of the young in the traditions of their families and ancestors? Genetically conditioned adaptedness will gradually be dissipated for at least two reasons. First, inept progeny will be pressed to follow their parents' careers despite the genetic incapacity. Second, whatever natural selection may have operated in the formation of the caste gene pool will probably be modified, abandoned, and perhaps even reversed.

Wastage of talent is, in fact, a fatal vice of all caste and rigid class systems. When social mobility is interdicted or seriously impeded, individuals qualified by their abilities to enter a given occupation are not admitted, and unqualified ones are retained. As the class structure becomes more open, impediments to social mobility decrease, and the principle of meritocracy becomes dominant. One's status and role in a society are acquired and not inherited from the parents. What may seem surprising at first is that when social inheritance of role and status becomes less influential, the importance of biological inheritance increases. This is a consequence of the genetic conditioning of those human characteristics which determine social mobility in open-class societies.

In a meritocracy, one's socioeconomic situation is a function of one's ability and achievement, rather than, or at least in addition to, inherited wealth or lack thereof. Educational institutions become channels of social mobility. Scholastic success is a function of aptitude and of willingness to exercise it, and aptitude is in part genetically conditioned. Since education and socioeconomic position are highly correlated, the status and material rewards are also indirectly genetically conditioned. Herrnstein (1971) puts this bluntly: "In addition to everything else, a high IQ pays in money." He offers the following syllogism as a clincher: "If differences in mental abilities are inherited, and if success requires those abilities, and if earnings and prestige depend on success, then social standing (which reflects earnings and prestige) will be based to some extent on inherited differences among people."

Have we arrived, in a roundabout way, at the conclusion so precious to race and class bigots, that the rich and the poor, the mighty and the humble, the elites and the reprobates, are where there genes have placed them? This is a misleading oversimplification. One must, first of all, distinguish two parts of the problem: the social status achieved by an adult person or a group of persons, and the choice of careers and ascription of status in their offspring. Excepting only the most rigid caste societies, the adult members of a society have always passed through some kind of social selective process. Their occupations, prestige, and positions on the social ladder reflect at least to some extent their abilities, conditioned by their environmental opportunities or by their genes—it does not matter which for the present argument. The question that now logically presents itself is this: To what extent does the social position of the offspring reflect the abilities of the parental or of the filial generation? Customs in many societies encourage, and often compel, children to follow the footsteps of their parents. Parental emotional impulses make the parents exert efforts to ease the ways of access for their children toward occupations and careers considered desirable or worthy. To the extent that these customs and impulses hold sway, the selective process is frustrated. This may happen even with apparently quite fair competitions, as in competitive tests and examinations for admission to certain schools. To what extent is the success or failure due to the intrinsic abilities of the examinees, or to the advantages and handicaps of their home environments and upbringing? This may not matter greatly to the selectors, if the purpose of the selection process is to obtain a group of individuals best able to profit from certain training. This is not so for the selectees and for the society as a whole, since many highly capable individuals are kept from admission to training and careers in which they could excel.

At this point one should be reminded of a basic fact of genetics which is all too often ignored. An individual's physical and mental constitutions are emergent products, not a mere sum of independent effects of his genes. Genes interact with each other, as well as with the environment. A gene B may enhance some desirable quality in combination with another gene A_1, but may have no effect or unfavorable effects with a gene A_2. Such nonadditive (epistatic) effects may be important determiners of intelligence, personality, special abilities, and other mental traits. For this reason, as well as because of the regression toward the mean, it is not at all rare that talented parents produce some mediocre offspring, and vice versa.

Assume, for the sake of argument, that at a certain time in history four castes or rigid socioeconomic classes are formed, composed initially of persons of demonstrated intellectual prowess (scholars), refined aesthetic discrimination (artists), physical valor or bravery (warriors), and luxury-loving social parasites. Assume further that these qualities were due to training and circumstances as well as to genetic conditioning. Shall we then have these four castes perpetuating themselves from generation to generation, with their respective characteristics unchanged? This is doubtful, for several reasons. It is highly unlikely that everybody in the original (founding) population of every caste carried the same genes, and even less likely that they were homozygous for these genes. The same degree of achievement in a given field can be due to diverse genetic endowments. Genetic (Mendelian) segregation will, therefore, generate from generation to generation an increasingly greater variety of genetic endowments, many of which will not equal or even approach those of the founders. Add to this the unlikelihood of absolute endogamy in any human population. A trickle, or even a stream, of foreign genes will gradually but inevitably dilute the original gene pool of the founders. For these reasons, all kinds of talent, excellence, and even genius arise throughout the social edifice. They appear on all socio-economic levels, even though they may be more likely in a statistical sense to be found in some than in other places. But a human being is a unique and nonrecurrent person, not a statistic; he deserves to be judged on his own merits, not according to the merits or demerits of his relatives.

Most discussions of genetic aspects of social stratification tacitly assume the value systems and political orders of modern quasidemocratic and meritocratic societies. It is a moot point whether the same kind of intelligence that leads to social preferment in these societies would do so everywhere. Modern China seems to be bent, not on searching for, but on abolition of elites, and on a radical leveling down of all socioeconomic disparities (Singer and Galston, 1972). If this is so, then either submissiveness and docility, or utter selflessness and ant-like dedication to the interests of the society as a whole, are now requisite for survival in something like a quarter of all mankind. It is wise to suspend judgment on whether the Chinese system will work out better or worse than ours.

A limited number of vacancies on the upper and intermediate levels of the social pyramid are available to much greater numbers of claimants in open-class societies, of the capitalist as well as of the Soviet communist kinds. A cutthroat competition takes place for the occupation of these vacancies. One wonders how often the winners in this competition are really best as human beings. Caste and rigid-class societies unforgivably wasted genetic talent and ability when these appeared among the lower orders of society. But it must be admitted that such societies did lessen the obnoxious aspects of competition. There is something to be said for the old-fashioned aristocrat who could afford to be gracious and magnanimous because he knew that his status was secure without contest.

Another tacit assumption should be brought into the open. Evaluation of scholastic ability and achievement usually takes for granted the educational system established in a given country. Those who succeed are rated superior and those who fail inferior. But is it possible that part of the blame should be charged to the educational system rather than to those who fail to pass the tests satisfactorily? It is well known, particularly to animal and plant breeders, that carriers of different genetic constitutions may respond most favorably to different environments. This is probably even more true of human genetic endowments. Ideally, every child should receive the environment most conducive to the development of his own particular abilities. Heber (1968) shows that spectacular improvements in manifested ability can be secured at the cost of concentrated effort. To what extent the ideal can be translated into practice is another matter. Some abilities may be judged more important than others in a given society. It must nevertheless be recognized that when everybody is put through the same educational machine, the abilities of many people will be grievously misjudged.

Genetic Sequelae of Perfect Equality

A decade ago (Dobzhansky, 1962) I attempted to envisage the genetic processes in a society with complete equality of opportunity for all its members. I was aware that this borders on utopia, but in recent years "futurology" has become something of a fashion among many social as well as natural scientists. The matter deserves a more detailed consideration.

A model of full equality of opportunity and of social mobility, favored by some sociologists, has been justly criticized by Eckland (1967). The model implicitly assumes that human ability is only environmentally determined and is randomly distributed in all socioeconomic strata. Full equality would then mean that identical proportions of children born to parents of different strata must enter any given occupation and achieve any given income level. Eckland points out that with this model "we would have to accept the unrealistic idea that, biologically, there is no more resemblance between a child and his parents than between a child and a total stranger."

In point of fact, people vary in their capacities to take advantage of opportunities that they meet, and these capacities are in part genetically conditioned. It appears undeniable that, in western postindustrial, quasi-democratic and meritocratic societies, IQ scores are fairly accurate predictors not only of scholastic but also of occupational achievement and, at a further remove, of income level and social status. Free mobility and perfect equality would then mean a perfect correspondence among intelligence, occupation, and status in a given society. Scarr-Salapatek (1971a) describes the resulting paradox as follows: "The greater the environmental equality, the greater the hereditary differences between levels in the social structure. The thesis of egalitarianism surely leads to its antithesis in a way that Karl Marx never anticipated." Liberals, progressives, egalitarians strove for abolition of class privilege and for equality of opportunity. The outcome, in capitalist as well as in socialist societies, would seem to be formation of genetically fixed classes. According to Eckland (1971), "In a completely open society under full equality of opportunity, a child's future position may be just as accurately predicted from the status of his biological parents as in a caste society. The basic difference between the two being that in a completely open system the causal links between generations would involve character specific or polygenic traits like intelligence, whereas in a caste system the links are consanguineous or cultural."

This sociogenetic model is an oversimplification. There is no denying that high-grade ability (whether genetically or environmentally conditioned) tends, in a meritocracy, to become concentrated in those positions which bring greater material rewards and prestige. It is, however, essential to keep in mind that human abilities are not only quantitatively but also qualitatively diversified. People achieve excellence in artistic, intellectual, administrative, political, athletic, commercial, and other pursuits and careers. It would be fatuous to rank these different pursuits in any order of increasing or decreasing merit. An individual engrossed in and dedicated to art may be uninterested in athletics, and vice versa. Yet equal material rewards and fame can be achieved in any one of these and other lines of endeavor. This is not contradicted by a statistical predictability of occupational and economic success from measurements of scholastic ability and achievement. It is not self-evident that a moderately low IQ (of course, not down to gross mental retardation levels) is a severe impediment for excellence in, say, baseball or boxing careers.

The concentration of human behavior geneticists on IQ studies is justified because the IQ, whatever its other defects, is measurable. But it is apt to obscure the fact that other, and perhaps equally heritable, characteristics and abilities play significant roles in choice of and success in different occupations. How about persistence, willingness to work, originality, creativity, leadership, ability to get along well with others, and plain human decency? Information available on the genetic conditioning of these abilities is fragmentary and inconclusive, and yet what information there is suggests that they may perhaps be grounded in the genetic endowment. Equal socioeconomic levels can be reached, in a meritocracy, by means of proficiency or excellence in quite diverse fields, provided that they are recognized in the society as useful. A mathematical genius may achieve fame, high status, and reasonably high income where there are universities and academies, but not in a tribe of hunters and gatherers. In some of the latter, the ability to go into trance or hypnotic state is valued highly (whether or not the latter ability is genetically conditioned is a different problem). Status and income are not absolutely correlated. Though most people like to have both a high status and a high income, some are more strongly attracted by the former and others by the latter. Examples are clergymen (relatively high status) and morticians (relatively high income).

Equality of opportunity has, then, two aspects. First, everybody is entitled to have access to the whole range of status and economic levels, regardless of the status or level of his parents and relatives. "Access" means that anyone may choose to strive and compete, or not to compete, for any position in the society; obviously it does not mean that the desired position will always be achieved. This depends on the adequacy of one's qualifications for that position. The wrong of caste and rigid class societies is that people are arbitrarily barred from access to a great many positions.

The second, and less evident, condition of equality of opportunity involves recognition that different people, carrying different genetic endowments, require different environments for their self-realization. A potential musical virtuoso is denied opportunity to develop his powers if he is prevented from entering a conservatory of music and is obliged instead to undergo the same training as, for example, future engineers. Ideal equality would entail provision of a set of diverse educational paths which people will choose, or be recommended to take, in accord with their tastes and abilities. In practice, this raises a host of thorny sociological and ethical problems. Is it inevitable that some children and youths will be selected as fit prospects for occupations or positions which are regarded for various reasons as more desirable, and others will be designated as lacking any particular talents? This can easily become a disguised form of social privilege.

Is there an escape from this impasse? It seems that it can only be found in some variant form of the socialist principle: "From each according to his abilities, to each according to his needs." This is not necessarily impossible to achieve in nonsocialist societies as well. Gross inequalities in material rewards may be eschewed. After all, some redistribution of wealth, making it more equal and equitable, has been going on in most technologically advanced countries for at least half a century (provoking cries of "creeping socialism" in some quarters). Perhaps equally important is avoidance of gross inequalities of status. This is at least in part a matter of ethics; an office or plant chief need not treat the janitors and charwomen with snobbish condescension.

And yet it is desirable and even indispensable for a society that those who possess rare or unusual abilities in some fields be induced to strive to achieve excellence in those fields. This usually means a more prolonged and arduous training than is requisite for more common and simpler occupations. Is it only desire of greater economic and status rewards that induces people to devote themselves to pursuit of outstanding achievement? With many people this is so, but with others achievement is self-rewarding. A musician, a poet, a craftsman, an athlete, and even a scientist and a politician derive a high degree of satisfaction and happiness from their works when they feel that their products are turning out well. It is not unheard of for people to turn down offers of greater economic rewards for the sake of being left free to pursue their favorite endeavors. It is not inconceivable that a day will be reached when the greatest monetary rewards will go to those engaged in socially indispensable but disagreeable work, such as garbage disposal, while those in occupations that tend to be self-rewarding may have to rest content with smaller emoluments.

Freedom of choice of training and occupation may entail wastage of effort and society's resources. Somebody striving to be a poet may turn out to be at most a poetaster, and an ambition to become a scientist may end in one's becoming a humdrum technician. Dashed hopes are painful to the person concerned, but denial of the right even to aspire for admission to some opportunities in a rigid class society is far more devastating. Any organization of society set up by fallible humans will fall short of perfection, but I firmly believe that one should work for as near an approach to full equality of opportunity and of status as can be secured. The two aspects of equality discussed above are indispensable: the ability freely to choose the goal of one's life and the direction of one's efforts, and the provision of a variety of environments, and of kinds of upbringing and training, suitable for diverse endowments of different persons.

Socioeconomic Classes or Aptitude Aggregations?

It cannot be overstressed that it is not the purpose of human equality to make everybody alike. Quite the opposite—it is a practical recognition that every individual is different from every other, and that every person is entitled to follow the path of his own choosing (provided he causes no injury to others).

Human genetic diversity is not a misfortune or a defect of human nature. It is a treasure with which the evolutionary process has endowed the human species. The companion treasure is the genetically conditioned educability, trainability, or malleability of human beings. Any human society, from the most primitive to the most complex (the latter more than the former), needs a diversity of men adapted and trained for a diversity of functions. Caste societies attempted, and failed, to achieve the requisite diversity by exploiting the real or imaginary genetic differences among men. Whether or not the diversity could be achieved in a meritocratic society by differential training if all men were genetically as similar as monozygotic twins is questionable. In reality, the diversity is obtained by a combination of genetic and environmental conditioning. The functionalist paradigm widely accepted in modern sociology assumes that "a key requisite for an operating social system is a relatively stable system of social rankings. . . . Given this assuption, an ongoing system of stratification requires a general set of ideological justifications. There must be various mechanisms which explain, justify, and propagate the system of inequality, and which cause men to accept as legitimate the fact of their own inequality. From an ideal-typical point of view, a system of stratification that is stable would set for various groups within societies goals that could be achieved by all within each group" (Lipset, 1968).

Equality is necessary if a society wishes to maximize the

benefits of genetic diversity among its members. With any-thing approaching full equality, every trade, craft, occupa-tion, and profession will concentrate within itself those who are genetically most fit for these roles. Will these aggrega-tions of genetic aptitudes amount to restoration of classes or even castes? The aptitude aggregations may develop into novel social phenomena, barely foreshadowed at present.

Critics of the functionalist paradigm have pointed out "that systems of stratification persist and take the varying forms they do because the privileged strata have more power and are able to impose their group interests on the society. . . . The value systems related to stratification therefore reflect the functional needs of the dominant strata, not those of the social system as such" (Lipset, 1968). The aptitude aggregations will differ from the old classes before all else by their fluidity. An aggregation will be gaining new members who are not descendants of the old members, probably in every generation. The gains will be more or less offset by losses of some of the progeny of the old members, who will pass to other aggregations. The gains and losses may be due in part to some occupations becoming more or less attrac-tive, or more or less socially important, so that more or fewer people are willing to be trained for them. Other gains and losses are genetically conditioned, and hence genetically significant. They result from segregation of Mendelian genes, and should not be frustrated by the "natural" and emotion-ally understandable impulses of parents to make their chil-dren inherit their occupations and status, or to propel them into what is regarded as more privileged occupations and status.

It is unlikely that the aptitude aggregation of, for example, musicians could have every member homozygous for the same gene for music, even if such a gene existed. The genetic basis of musical talent is probably a constellation of several genes, and possibly different genes in different persons. It is even less likely that every spouse of every musician is homozygous for the same gene or genes. Some of the progeny in families of musicians will, then, lack conspicuous musical talents, and will pass to other professional aggregations. Conversely, some talented musicians are born in families of these other aggregations, and will be absorbed in the aggregation of musicians. This is analogous to the present interclass social mobility, but more closely tied to genetic processes in human populations. Moreover, the mobility should not be conceived as unidirectional but as multidirectional. Instead of moving up or down a single socioeconomic scale, the exchange of persons and of genes occurs between more or less numerous functional aggregations, some of which are economically equivalent.

Children of musicians, or athletes, or intellectuals grow up in environments in which musicianship, or athletics, or intellectual pursuits are likely to be appreciated and encouraged. Although not every offspring in such families inherits the genes that condition the respective talents or inclinations, the probability of talented individuals being born in such families is greater than in other families. Furthermore, the genetic consequences of assortative matings should not be underestimated. The genes for a certain kind of aptitude are found scattered in all social strata and in all professional aggregations. Nevertheless, the marriage of individuals who carry genes for similar aptitudes will occur more often than would be expected by chance alone. Assortative matings need not be due to conscious choice, but may be rather a matter of propinquity. Statistically speaking, families engaged in similar occupations are more likely to be acquainted than those in different occupations. My wife and I were once surprised to find that more than 90 percent of persons on the list of our acquaintances were either themselves engaged, or were married to persons engaged, in academic professions. Schools, colleges, and universities function as assortative marriage brokers simply by bringing together young people of similar interests and roughly similar abilities (Eckland, 1970).

The genetic consequences of positive assortative mating have not been adequately analyzed genetically. Considered formally, assortative mating promotes increased homozygosis for the genes that determine the charactistics involved in the choice of mates. The most interesting and significant aspect from the standpoint of human societies is the increase in variance in the populations in which assortative matings frequently occur. Most human aptitudes form graded continua, and are conditioned by several genes reinforcing each other's action. Some people are tone-deaf and find music a nuisance, others are mediocre or fairly good, still others are excellent musicians, and there are also geniuses, like Bach or Beethoven. With random mating, and with genes conditioning a given ability scattered in the population, the likelihood of many of these genes coming together by chance is relatively small. It is increased when the carriers of these genes are more likely to mate with each other than with noncarriers. The aptitude aggregations formed under equality of opportunity would lead inevitably to positive assortative mating. This will not necessarily yield a bumper crop of geniuses (too little is known about the genetic bases of human abilities for such predictions), but the probability of such events is enhanced.

Conclusions

It is hardly surprising that equality is not welcomed by everybody. Some biologists have managed to concoct horrendous tales of its supposedly dysgenic consequences. Equality has, allegedly, drained the lower classes of genetic talents that were occasionally found there in the good old days of class societies which discouraged social mobility. What remains at the bottom of the socioeconomic ladder are worthless dregs. This fantasy is easily dispelled by considering how recent are tentative attempts at equality of opportunity, even in socially advanced societies. However, there is a real sociogenetic problem which should not be lost sight of because we reject the fantasy. We have seen that, in a society approaching full equality of opportunity, there will be formed diverse aggregations of people, concentrating different genetic aptitudes. Is it realistic to envisage a society consisting entirely of such elite aggregations? Or will there be left over a large aggregation devoid of any particular aptitudes, except for occasional birth of some elite gene constellations?

Given the present state of ignorance of human behavior genetics, it would be folly to propound dogmatic answers to the above questions. I agree with Scarr-Salapatek (1971a) that differences between humans "can simply be accepted as differences and not as deficits. If there are alternate ways of being successful within the society, then differences can be valued variations on the human theme regardless of their environmental or genetic origins." People need not be branded elites and commonality. Increasing equality of status and economic equality must complement equality of opportunity. Manual labor is not intrinsically inferior to intellectual labor, even though more people may be adept at the former than at the latter. Efforts to uncover rare abilities need not detract from appreciation of more common ones. All this is admittedly hard to accept for those who were brought up in class societies or in societies that encourage unrestrained competition for status. I feel, however, that this is ethically desirable, and, moreover, that history is moving ineluctably in this direction.

Finally, again one must stress that the diversity we observe is a joint product of genetic and environmental differences. The observed diversity is, in principle, controllable by genetic as well as by environmental means. The more that becomes known about the causes that underlie the diversity, the greater the possibilities of control. This is the ultimate purpose and justification of scientific research in biology, psychology, and sociology. A considerable part of mankind, from city slums of the richest country in the world to the inhabitants of the have-not countries, are at present deprived not only of optimal but of simply tolerable conditions for physical and mental development. This part of mankind must be helped to secure such conditions. It is hypocrisy to say that their deprivations come from their inferior genes, and must be corrected by eugenic elimination of these genes. Eugenics will eventually come into its own. But, as Osborn (1968) has pointed out, eugenic amelioration can only be successful given antecedent environmental and sociological improvements.

EVOLUTIONARY GENETICS
OF RACE

"I T IS NOT my intention here to describe the several so-called races of men; but to inquire what is the value of the differences between them under a classificatory point of view, and how they have originated." This is Darwin's sentence opening the chapter "On the Races of Man" in *The Descent of Man* (1871). A century later, it remains appropriate to open a discussion of the races of man in the light of genetics with the same sentence. Despite the enormous growth of information concerning racial variation in man as well as in other organisms, the problems which occupied Darwin are still at issue. In a sense, the incertitudes have increased. It is the contention of a small but vociferous group of students that mankind is not differentiated into races. Even if this contention were justified, which I believe is not the case, our discussion would not lose its point. If mankind has no races, it is surely not homogeneous or uniform. The diversity would still have to be described, studied, and explained.

Genetic diversity among humans is a matter of far more than theoretical or academic interest. It has great many sociopolitical implications. Race diversity is a form of genetic diversity that is often involved in sociopolitical debates. All too frequently, strong biases and partisan feelings are elicited by a mere mention of "race problems." The biological phenomenon of races within the human species appears to be more complex than are races in sexually reproducing and outbreeding species of animals and plants. This is because human races are subject to cultural as well as to biological influences. The greatest trouble is that the study of races in man is beclouded by partisan bigotries. An "ivory tower" scientist prefers to stay away from problems which arouse such emotional biases. And yet, the human importance of the many issues relevant to race is too great to allow the problem to be held in abeyance, or to be given a free run by the bigots. Clarification of biological and other aspects of the race phenomenon is greatly needed.

Individual and Group Diversity

Immanuel Kant, who was a naturalist before he became the prince of philosophers, wrote in 1775 the following remarkably perceptive lines: "Negroes and whites are not different species of humans (they belong presumably to one stock), but they are different races, for each perpetuates itself in every area, and they generate between them children that are necessarily hybrid, or blending (mulattoes). On the other hand blonds and brunets are not different races of whites, for a blond man can also get from a brunette woman, altogether blond children, even though each of these deviations maintains itself throughout protracted generations under any and all transplantations."

Kant understood the distinction between individual (*intra*populational) and group (*inter*populational) variabilities more clearly than do some modern authors. In our modern terminology, the situation can be described as follows. Excepting only monozygotic twins and other multiple births, any two individuals differ in several, probably many, genes. Parents and children, siblings, more remote relatives, and people not known to be related, differ, on the average, in more and more genes. A person's genotype is unique, unprecedented, and nonrecurrent. As shown in the first chapter of this book, the proximate source of individual genetic variability is Mendelian segregation in sexually reproducing and outbreeding populations. An individual is heterozygous for many (probably thousands or tens of thousands) of his genes. No two sex cells that he produces are likely to contain the same identical sets of genes; the sex cells of his mate are equally diversified; the zygotes (children) which they bring forth will be, on the average, heterozygous for and different in as many genes as their parents were.

With group variability, the units of study are no longer individuals, but biologically and genetically connected arrays of individuals—populations. It rarely happens that every individual of a population A differs in the same way from every individual of the population B, and the arrays A and B consist of genetically identical individuals. Such a situation does occur in organisms, chiefly but not exclusively some groups of plants and microorganisms, in which the prevalent or obligatory methods of reproduction are asexual fission, budding, diploid parthenogenesis, or self-pollination. Thousands or even millions of individuals among such organisms belong to the same clone (result of asexual reproduction) or pure line (self-pollination), and may have the same genotypes. These are, indeed, "pure races." The inhabitants of a territory can be described by listing which pure races occur there, and specifying their relative frequencies. To cite a single example, Allard and Kannenberg (1968) found in central California at least eight pure lines of the self-pollinating grass *Festuca microstachys*; the relative frequencies of these lines differ from locality to locality, apparently depending on which lines are best adapted to the environments of a particular locality.

To describe human populations in terms of the proportions of different "pure races" or "types" has been a dream of some physical anthropologists, and this dream dies hard (see Dobzhansky, 1970). But it is a pipe dream, because mankind is, and always was, a sexually reproducing and outbreeding species. Excepting monozygotic multiple births, it has and can have no clones, no pure lines, and no pure races. It consists of genetically unique individuals. False leads to the dreamland of "pure races" have nevertheless abounded. It would be so nice to be able to tell to what pure race every individual belongs!

Human populations are polymorphic for eye and hair

colors, blood groups, and many other traits. Could one declare blue-eyed persons to constitute one race and brown-eyed another? Or may one race include the possessors of blood group O, another of A, and the third of B? This would be ludicrous; parents and children, as well as siblings, would often find themselves belonging to different races. Equally meaningless races of criminals, aristocrats, or people suffering from tuberculosis or other diseases have been discussed and written about. The fallacy is that the groups of people concerned are not populations in the biological sense, but collections of individuals arbitrarily selected according to single traits. After all, criminals are born mostly to parents who are not criminals, and some of their offspring are not criminals either. There probably is a genetic predisposition to tuberculosis, but people suffering from this disease are not a breeding community separate from healthy ones. Except in a caste system, no aristocracy or ruling elite is a Mendelian population separate from the plebeians.

The notions of pure races and of Platonic types or ideas are lurking in the background of various taxonomies of constitutional types. Kretschmer's pyknic, athletic, and asthenic body builds and associated psychological types are admittedly rare in their extreme or pure forms. Nevertheless, they can be perceived among the manifold products of the general miscegenation in which mankind has been engaged for centuries and millennia. Sheldon's 88 somatotypes are combinations of graded series of three supposedly independent variables—endomorphy, mesomorphy, and ectomorphy. The genetics of these variables is obscure. If there existed series of multiple alleles in each of the three genes, for endomorphy, mesomorphy, and ectomorphy, the 88 somatotypes

could be interpreted as an elaborate instance of intrapopulational polymorphism. This remains to be demonstrated.

For more than half of a century, the Polish school of anthropology consistently adhered to strictly typological assumptions (see the reviews by Czekanowski, 1962, the
venerable dean of this school, and also Wiercinski, 1962, and
Bielicki, 1962). Populations are described in terms of the
incidence in them of racial "types," which are "distinguished
by diagnosing the racial affinities of individuals independently
of their ethnic origins." European populations are composed
of Nordic, Mediterranean, Armenoid, and Lapponoid races
or racial types. The frequencies of these types in each population are given with a precision to one-tenth of 1 percent,
as though men belonged to one or another clone or pure
line, like *Festuca microstachys* grasses (see above). Mediterranean individuals in the Polish, Swiss, and Italian populations are assumed to be more alike than any of these
is to his Nordic or Armenoid neighbors or brothers. Michalski
and Wiercinski can identify as many as 16 "racial elements"
of which mankind is a composite. Each of these races, or
types, or elements is recognized by a constellation of chiefly
morphological traits, such as stature, eye and hair color,
hair form, cephalic, orbital, and facial and nasal indices. A
set of mathematical techniques has been devised to identify
to which racial type every individual belongs. Can this really
be accomplished? As with biological mathematics generally,
the results of even the most precise and elaborate calcula-
tions do no more than give numerical expressions of the biological assumptions put at the base of the mathematical
model. These assumptions in the present case, insofar as they
have been stated at all, are untenable. The crucial assump-

tion is that the trait constellations which supposedly identify the Nordic, Armenoid, Lapponoid, and so on, racial types are inherited as alleles of a single gene, somewhat like those giving O, A, and B blood groups. This is in flat contradiction to all that is known about the genetics of these traits. Wiercinski (1962) gives an example of a family in which the father is diagnosed as Alpine, the mother as Nordic, and their two children as Lapponoid and Nordic. This stretches one's credulity to the breaking point.

Mendelian Populations

A person has two parents, four grandparents, eight great-grandparents, and so on. Continued for some 33 generations, the number of ancestors turns out greater than the total world population. Of course, this is impossible. Notwithstanding the universality of incest taboos, all our ancestors were more or less distant relatives. Though this cannot be documented, all humans are relatives. If one could construct a complete pedigree of all mankind, it would be a complex network on which every individual is multiply related to every other. Mankind is a complex Mendelian population, a reproductive community all members of which are connected by ties of mating and parentage. A Mendelian population has a common gene pool. The genes of every individual are derived from, and unless he dies childless some of them return to, this pool.

In theory, mankind could be described by listing its gene loci, and indicating the frequencies in the gene pool of the different alleles at each locus. Such a description, even if it were possible in practice, would not be entirely satisfactory.

Mankind is not a panmictic population, in which every individual would have an equal probability of mating with every individual of the opposite sex and of the appropriate age. The chance is greater that a boy born in Canada will marry a Canadian girl rather than a girl from China or Uganda. In common with many sexually reproducing animal and plant species, mankind is differentiated geographically into subordinate Mendelian populations; intermarriage within these subordinate populations is more frequent than between them. There are also specifically human agencies which cause further discontinuities in the intermarriage patterns, such as economic, social class, linguistic, religious, and other subdivisions.

Mankind, the biological species, is the inclusive Mendelian population. Within it is a hierarchy of subordinate Mendelian populations, geographically or socially partially isolated from each other. Only the smallest subdivisions, inhabitants of some villages, groups of equal social status in small towns, may be regarded as approximately panmictic. Races are subordinate Mendelian populations within a species. They are not Platonic or statistical types, not collections of genetically identical individuals, and not subdivisions of primordial mankind submerged by lengthy miscegenation. They are Mendelian populations which differ in the incidence of some genes in their gene pools.

Delimitation of the Mendelian population of the human species as a whole presents no difficulty. At our time level there is no gene exchange between the gene pool of the human species and that of even its closest biological relatives, pongids or anthropoid apes. It is sometimes asked how one defines a human being. Biologically, the answer is simple: any individual is human whose genes are derived from the gene pool of the human species. By contrast, delimitation of the Mendelian populations which are called races is always to some extent vague, because their gene pools are not wholly disjunct. This is a restatement in modern terms of Darwin's conclusion that "The most weighty of all arguments against treating the races of man as distinct species, is that they graduate into each other, independently in many cases, as far as we can judge, of their having intercrossed."

The subordinate, intraspecific, Mendelian populations, in man as well as in other sexual organisms, are as a rule not fully discrete. Because of gene exchange, they merge into each other. Very often one cannot tell where one ends and the other begins. Even for the major human races (yellow, white, black, and red), frankly intermediate populations occur which defy all attempts of placing them into one or the other of these pigeonholes (for example, are the Turkic-speaking tribes of Central Asia yellow or white?). With the finer geographic, linguistic, or economic subdivisions, the boundaries of the subordinate Mendelian populations are even more blurred, because intermarriage and gene exchange between them occurs increasingly often.

The lack of sharp boundaries between subordinate Mendelian populations in man is disconcerting to some orderly minds. How can one make something so ill-defined the basic unit of biological and anthropological study? Two observations can be made in this connection. First, the complexities of the order of nature should not be evaded. Second, the only way to simplify nature is to study it as it is, not as we would have liked it to be.

Gene Exchange

Biologically basic, and until the advent of culture the only factor maintaining (though not in itself producing) the genetic differentiation of intraspecific Mendelian populations, was isolation by distance.* This phenomenon is very complex, and still far from adequately understood. Probably the most penetrating analyses thus far are those of Wright (a detailed summary and review of the literature in Wright, 1969). Three models have been suggested. Mathematically the most tractable is the "island" model; the other two are isolation by distance over a uniform inhabited area, and the "stepping-stone" model. The island model assumes that the species consists of discrete colonies within which panmixia prevails, but which receive the proportion, *m*, of immigrants drawn at random from the rest of the species. The isolation of the islands may vary in space and in time, the value of *m* ranging from zero (complete isolation) to one (no isolation). If the immigrants come (as they usually do) from the neighboring colonies, rather than from the species

---

* Isolation by distance, or geographical isolation, should not be confused with reproductive isolating mechanisms, which act as barriers against gene exchange between incipient or full species. Reproductive isolation is by definition genetic. For example, ethological isolation, lack of sexual attraction between females of one and males of another species, is conditioned by some of the gene differences between these species. So is hybrid inviability and hybrid sterility. By contrast, geographically isolated populations, such as those inhabiting different islands, may, in principle, be genetically identical. Even if they are not genetically identical, the differences between them need not be responsible for their geographical separation. Only ecological isolation, genetically conditioned preference for different habitats, is in a sense intermediate between geographic and reproductive isolation.

at large, we have the stepping-stone model. This merges into the situation in which the distribution area of the species is inhabited continuously and uniformly, but the mobility of individuals is limited, so that the parents come from a more or less small fraction of the total area.

Situations conforming to all three models, as well as intermediate states, are found in man. Cavalli-Sforza (1959; and Cavalli-Sforza and Bodmer, 1970) studied the "matrimonial migration" among towns and villages of the Parma diocese in northern Italy, and Harrison (1967) studied villages in Orfordshire in England. The bride and groom may be inhabitants of the same village, or the mates may be from different villages. Both authors found that the probability of marriage is a negative exponential function of the distance between the villages in which the potential mates reside. It is also a function of the numbers of inhabitants in the villages; the greater the population of a village, the more potential mates it contains. Harrison's data for the marriage distances in the population of the parish of Charlton, according to the statistics of 1861, show that places within one mile from Charlton contributed some 55 mates per 1,000 inhabitants, while places four or more miles away contributed five mates or fewer.

An important factor in matrimonial migration, and consequently in the gene flow between Mendelian populations, is not only physical distance but also facility of travel. Cavalli-Sforza found the following distribution of marriage distances among the inhabitants of level and mountainous parts of the Parma diocese in Italy (Table 2–1).

The mobility among the inhabitants of the plain is greater, except perhaps at distances of more than 42 units, than

TABLE 2-1

Matrimonial distances in percentages among the inhabitants of the plain (P) and mountainous (M) parts of the Parma diocese (after Cavalli-Sforza, 1959).

Distance	P	M
0– 2.5	51.3	64.2
2.5– 6.5	9.9	9.9
6.5–12.5	15.2	6.6
12.5–20.5	9.9	6.3
20.5–30.5	6.0	3.9
30.5–42.5	3.7	1.8
> 42.5	3.7	6.7

NOTE: A unit distance is 0.625 km.

among the mountaineers. Cavalli-Sforza and Bodmer (1970) have correlated this greater mobility, and also the greater population density on the plain than in the mountains, with genetic differentiation of the village populations. Common genetic markers, OAB, MN, and Rh blood types, have been recorded in the populations. No significant differences between the villages of the plain were found, while an appreciable heterogeneity was brought to light among the mountain villages. The highest heterogeneity was observed in the parishes ("comune") with lowest population densities.

Neel (1969) and his collaborators carried out gene frequency studies of 25 different gene loci in 39 villages of the Yanomama tribe of American Indians on the Upper Orinoco in Venezuela. Very appreciable diversities have been recorded for several loci (R^2 from 0 to 0.11, MS from 0 to 0.21, P^1 from 0.34 to 0.70, Jk^a from 0.38 to 0.84). Cavalli-Sforza ascribes the heterogeneities to random genetic drift rather than to local differences in natural selection. Neel interprets "these differences as primarily reflecting the manner in which new villages originate." However that may be, the role of gene exchange between local populations as a genetically leveling factor is quite apparent.

Gene Gradient or Clines

The above are examples of *micro*geographic differentiation of Mendelian populations of the human species. Man is a social animal; his settlement patterns and the reproductive biology of human populations sometimes permit genetic difference to arise among geographically adjacent population nuclei. We now turn to the *macro*geographic differentiation, which is quantitatively but probably not qualitatively distinct from the microgeographic. For some tens of thousands of years, mankind has been a nearly cosmopolitan species. Human populations live under a variety of physical and cultural environments. Although man has always been a wanderer, and his traveling ability has increased enormously owing to the progress of his technology, some populations are separated by distances so great that the gene exchange between them is limited. Populations that inhabit different continents and parts of the same continent often differ in many genes; as a consequence, they differ in many morphological and physiological characteristics. In other words, mankind is an aggregate of racially distinct populations.

The genetic nature of the race differences is only beginning to be understood. The classical race concept, in anthropology as well as in biology, was typological. Every individual of Negroid, Mongoloid, Caucasoid, and even Jewish and Nordic "races" was a variant of a mythical "type" of his race.

Operationally, this concept led to characterization of the racial types by systems of average values of measurements and observations made on samples of populations living in, or descended from ancestors who resided in, different territories, or belonging to different castes, or speaking different languages. The more separate measurements or traits went into the construction of a racial type, the more valid and reliable it was supposed to be. This typological approach reached its extreme, almost a *reductio ad absurdum,* in the attempts discussed above to find different racial types among individuals of the same population, and even among members of the same family.

Genetics has gradually made the ineptitude of typological approaches evident to increasing majorities of anthropologists. Mendelian populations should be described in terms of the incidence in them of separate characteristics, and ideally of the alleles of variant genes. Boyd's (1950) pioneering attempt to carry out such a description using the then-known blood genes met a skeptical reception, although the race classification he arrived at was little different from some then-current typological ones. The two decades since have increased greatly the available information, and also revealed complexities that were not so clearly apparent before.

When the frequencies of gene alleles or of separate phenotypic traits are plotted on maps (see examples in Mourant, 1954; Mourant et al., 1958; Lundman, 1967), one finds as a rule gradients (clines) of increasing or decreasing frequencies toward or away from some centers. Thus, the allele *I^B* of the OBA blood group system reaches frequencies between 25 and 30 percent in central Asia and northern India.

Its frequencies decline westward to 15 to 20 percent in European Russia, 5 to 10 percent in western Europe, and even lower in parts of Spain and France. The frequencies also decline southeastward, practically to zero among Australian Aborigines, northeastward to below 10 percent among the Eskimos, and to zero in unmixed Amerindians. The center of light skin and eye pigmentation is northwestern Europe; the pigmentation becomes darker eastward and especially southward, reaching maximum in subsacharan Africa, southern India, and Melanesia. Rohrer's index (body weight divided by the height cubed) reaches highest values among the Eskimos, and is lowest in southern Asia, Australia, and Africa.

Are any genetic differences among human populations qualitative, in the sense that some gene alleles are absent in some and reach 100 percent frequencies in other populations? As noted by Darwin, "Of all the differences between the races of man, the color of the skin is the most conspicuous and one of the best marked." Indeed (cases of albinism excepted), no native of subsacharan Africa is born as lightly pigmented as the natives of Europe, and no European develops as dark a pigmentation as an African. However, this skin color difference is due to additive effects of at least three, possibly twice as many, pairs of genes without dominance. Heritable skin color variations are found among Europeans as well as among Africans. One can well imagine that the skin color could be darkened considerably by selective breeding in a population of European descent, and lightened in a population of African descent. Whether or not the *intra*racial pigment variations are due to the same gene loci which are responsible for the *inter*racial differences is uncertain. One of the alleles of the Rh system (*cDe*) reaches frequencies above 50 percent in African populations, but it occurs with low frequencies, generally below 5 percent, elsewhere in the world, in individuals without known African ancestry. An allele of the Diego locus seems to be lacking among Europeans and is frequent among Amerindians, although not reaching 100-percent frequencies among the latter. An allele of the Duffy system has frequencies above 90 percent among Negroes in western Africa, but is also found with low frequencies among Europeans.

Our tentative conclusion, subject to modification by future findings, must be that qualitative differences, in the sense defined above, are absent among human populations. This is in no way contradicted by our ability to distinguish any individual native in, for example, Congo or Ghana from any Scandinavian, and both of these from any native of eastern Asia. The reason is, of course, that the populations native in these countries differ in frequencies not of a single gene but of many genes. Typological race concepts must be replaced by populational ones. Individuals are not accidental departures from their racial types. On the contrary, interpopulational racial differences are compounded of the same genetic variants which are responsible for genetic differences among individuals within a population, and even among siblings and parents and children.

Racial Differences and Races Named

The apparently endless variety of living beings is as fascinating as it is perplexing. There are no two identical humans, as there are no two identical pine trees, or two Drosophila flies, or two infursoria. The runaway diversity of our perceptions is made manageable by means of human language. Classifying and giving names to classes of things is perhaps the primordial scientific activity. It may antedate the appearance of *Homo sapiens,* and it is bound to continue as long as symbol-forming animals will exist. Biologists and anthropologists describe and name the complexes of organisms which they study in order to identify for themselves, and let others know, what they are talking and writing about.

Human beings whom we meet, and about whose existence we learn from others, are numerous and diversified. We have to classify them and attach recognition labels to the classes. So we distinguish the speakers of English, Russian, Swahili, and other languages; college students, industrial workers, and farmers; intellectuals and the "silent majority," and so on. Those who study human physical, physiological, and genetic variations among men find it convenient to name races. Races can be defined as arrays of Mendelian populations belonging to the same biological species, but differing from each other in incidence of some genetic variants.

The question is often posed: Are races objectively ascertainable phenomena of nature, or are they mere group concepts invented by biologists and anthropologists for their convenience? Here we must make unequivocally clear the duality of the race concept. First, it refers to objectively ascertainable genetic differences among Mendelian populations. Second, it is a category of classification which must serve the pragmatic function of facilitating communication. One can specify the operational procedures whereby any two populations can be shown to be racially different or racially identical.

The populations contain different arrays of genotypes if racially different, or similar arrays if racially identical.

Racial differences exist between populations regardless of whether or not somebody is studying them. Yet this does not mean that any two genetically different populations must receive different race names. For example, Cavalli-Sforza (1959) has found no significant genetic differentiation between inhabitants of villages on the densely settled Parma plain; he did find such a differentiation between the villages in the more sparsely settled mountains (see above). Racial differences are, therefore, ascertained among the latter but not among the former. It would nevertheless not occur to anyone to give race names to the populations of every mountain village. The village names are adequate labels for the populations that live in them.

How many arrays of populations in the human species should be provided with race names is a matter of expediency. Already, Darwin noted that "Man has been studied more carefully than any other organic being, and yet there is the greatest possible diversity among capable judges" concerning the number of races recognized and named. Different authors referred to by Darwin named from 2 to as many as 63 races. The incertitude is undiminished today. Hardly any two independently working classifiers have proposed identical sets of races. This lack of unanimity has driven some modern "capable judges" to desperation. They claim that mankind has no races, and that the very word "race" should be expunged from the lexicon. This proposal is often motivated by a laudable desire to counteract notorious racist propaganda. But will this be achieved by denying the existence of races? Or will such denials only impair the credibility of the scientists making them? Is it not better to make people understand the nature of the race differences, rather than to pretend that such differences are nonexistent? To give an example of a race classification by an author fully conversant with modern biology and anthropology, Garn (1965) recognizes 9 "geographical races" and 32 "local races," some of the latter being subdivisions of the former. The geographical races are as follows:

1. Amerindian
2. Polynesian
3. Micronesian
4. Australian
5. Melanesian-Papuan
6. Asiatic
7. Indian
8. European
9. African

Among the local races not included in his major geographical list, Garn distinguishes three interesting categories —Ainu and Bushmen are "long-isolated marginal," Lapps, Pacific Negritos, African Pygmies, and Eskimos are "puzzling, isolated, numerically small," and American Blacks, Cape Colored, Ladinos, and Neo-Hawaiians are "hybrid local races of recent origin." On the other hand, Lundman (1967) recognizes only 4 main races—white, yellow, red (Amerindian), and black; his 16 subraces correspond only in part to Garn's local races. If one of these classifications is accepted as correct, must the other necessarily be incorrect? This, I believe, need not be so; we should rather ask which classification is more convenient, and for what purpose.

In sexually reproducing and outbreeding organisms, every individual can usually be recognized as a member of one and only one species, or else as a hybrid of two species. Adherents to the typological race concepts believed that the same should be true of races. Every individual, excepting only the progeny of interracial crosses, should be classifiable as belonging to a certain race. This is not so, because species are genetically closed, while races are genetically open systems. For example, there is no individual whose belonging to the species man or the species chimpanzee could be called in question. These species do not exchange genes. There are, however, many local populations in northwestern Asia intermediate between the white and the yellow, and in northern Africa intermediate between the white and the black races. This does not mean that individual members of these intermediate populations necessarily have two parents belonging to different "pure" white, black, or yellow races. Whole populations are intermediate. Sometimes this is due to secondary intergradation (Mayr, 1963), i.e., to interbreeding of populations which became genetically distinct in a near or remote past. This is, in fact, the origin of Garn's "hybrid local races." More often the intermediate populations are autochthonous; primary intergradation is a result of gene diffusion taking place while the racial divergence of the populations is in progress, as well as after the populations have diverged. The gene gradients or clines result from both primary and secondary intergradations.

Gene gradients make it only rarely possible to draw a line on the map to divide the regions of different races. Race boundaries are more often blurred than sharp. Worse still, gradients of the frequencies of different genes and traits may be only weakly or not at all correlated. This can easily be seen on maps that show the frequencies of various traits in human populations, such as different blood antigens, pigmentation, and stature (see, e.g., the maps in Lundman, 1967). Human races are not discrete units imagined by typologists, so some disappointed typologists have seen fit to draw the radical conclusion that races do not exist.

Let us take a closer look at the situation. If gene or character gradients were uniform, gene frequencies would increase or decrease regularly by so many percentages per so many miles traveled in a given direction. With uniform gradients, race boundaries could only be arbitrary. However, often the gradients are steeper in some places and are more gentle or absent elsewhere. Consider two gene alleles, A_1 and A_2, in a species with a distribution area 2,100 miles across. Suppose that for 1,000 miles the frequency of A_1 declines from 100 to 90 percent; for the next 100 miles from 90 to 10 percent; and for the remaining 1,000 miles from 10 to 0 percent. It is then reasonable and convenient to divide the species into two races, characterized by the predominance of A_1 and A_2, respectively, and to draw the geographic boundary between the races where the cline is steep.

Why are the gene frequency gradients gentle in some and steep in other places? The steepening of the gradients usually coincides with geographic and environmental barriers that make travel difficult. Barriers to travel are also barriers to gene diffusion. Newman (1963) has analyzed the human racial taxonomy in a thoughtful article. His general conclusion is that ". . . there are valid races among men, but that biology is only beginning to properly discover and define them. . . . I consider some of Garn's races probably valid, others probably invalid, with still others in the 'suspense' category for lack of adequate data." He validates Garn's Asiatic, African, and Amerindian races as showing good trait correlations in such visible traits as pigmentation, hair form and quantity, nose and lip form, cheek bone prominence, eyelid form, and general body shape. European, Indian, and Australian are "unwarranted abstractions," on account of the high variability and discordance (lack of correlation) in the geographical distribution of many traits. Melanesian, Polynesian, and Micronesian are in the "suspense" category.

Adherents of the "no races" school argue that one should study the geographic distributions of genes and character frequencies, rather than attempt to delimit races. The truth is that both kinds of studies are necessary. Gene and character geography is the basis of the biological phenomenon of racial variation; classification and naming are indispensable for information storage and communication. The fact that races are not always or even usually discrete, and that they are connected by transitional populations, is in itself biologically meaningful. This is evidence of gene flow between races being not only potentially possible but actually taking place. Gene flow between species, however, is limited or prevented altogether. To hold that because races are not rigidly fixed units they do not exist is a throwback to typological thinking of the most misleading kind. It is about as logical as saying that towns and cities do not exist because the country intervening between them is not totally uninhabited, or that youth and old age do not exist because there is also middle age.

Race Differences as Products of Natural and Sexual Selection

A century ago Darwin felt "baffled in all our attempts to account for the differences between the races of man." In particular, natural selection can hardly be invoked, because "we are at once met by the objection that beneficial variations alone can be thus preserved; and as far as we are enabled to judge (although always liable to error on this head) not one of the external differences between the races of man are of any direct or special service to him." He put more faith in sexual selection: "For my own part I conclude that of all the causes which have led to the differences in external appearance between the races of man, and to a certain extent between man and the lower animals, sexual selection has been by far the most efficient." Of the 828 pages of *The Descent of Man, and Selection in Relation to Sex,* part I, "On the Descent of Man," takes 250 pages, and part II, "Sexual Selection," more than twice as many.

It is almost incredible that, a century after Darwin, the problem of the origin of racial differences in the human species remains about as baffling as it was in his time. Several circumstances have conspired to make it so. The chief one was that, until less than a generation ago, the leading anthropologists assumed that race differences are mostly adaptively neutral, and consequently made little effort to discover their selective values. Radical changes in human environments brought about by cultural developments made the problem particularly difficult to approach; a genetic trait may have played an adaptive role a million years ago which was quite different from its role ten thousand years ago, and that again may have been different from what it is at present. Finally, by a curious twist of reasoning, the doctrine of human equality seemed to exclude the possibility of differential genetic adaptedness.

The adaptive significance of even so obvious a trait as

skin pigmentation has not been fully clarified. The notion that a dark pigmentation is protective against sunburn is very old, and made plausible by the fact that dark-skinned races are (or were) inhabitants of the tropics, and light-skinned ones of temperate and cold countries. This rule is not free of exceptions; the Indians of equatorial South America are not particularly dark, and some of the natives of northeastern Siberia are at least as dark as those of Mediterranean Europe. These exceptions have been "explained" by assuming that the relatively light people in the hot countries and the relatively dark ones in cold countries are recent immigrants, or that Indians of equatorial America live mostly in forest shade rather than in the open. It has also been supposed that light skins facilitate the synthesis of vitamin D in countries with little sunshine, while dark pigmentations protect against excessive amounts of this vitamin where the sunshine is abundant. There is good evidence that light skins are more prone to develop skin cancers owing to sun exposure than are dark skins. Still another surmise is that dark skin pigmentation may facilitate absorption of solar radiation "where energy must be expended to maintain body temperature, at as dawn and dusk in otherwise hot climates" (Hamilton and Heppner, 1967). Finally, a dark skin may give a protective coloration to a hunter stalking game or escaping from predators.

The above hypotheses concerning the adaptive significance of pigmentation are not mutually contradictory or exclusive, and yet their multiplicity attests to the inadequacy of our understanding of the adaptive role of even the most conspicuous of all human racial differences. A considerable amount of careful study has been devoted to the physiology of human populations adapted to certain particularly rigorous environments, such as Indians of the Andean Altiplano (cold, low oxygen supply), and Eskimos of the Arctic (Baker and Weiner, 1966; Baker et al., 1967). Riggs and Sargent (1964) and others compared the reactions of young black and white males to exertion under humid heat conditions. Some statistically assured differences in the expected directions have been found, but it is not ruled out that a part of these differences may be the product of physiological adaptation to the environments in which the person grew up.

Racial differences in the incidence of various blood groups have long been a challenge to those who believe that all racial differences must be established by natural selection. There is no doubt that certain pathological conditions (e.g., duodenal ulcers) occur more often in carriers of some blood antigens than in others, but it is questionable whether these correlations are even in small part responsible for the racial differences. Attempts to correlate the blood groups with resistance to some infectious diseases, such as plague, smallpox, and syphilis, have thus far been unconvincing (a review in Otten, 1967).

Sexual selection "depends on the advantage which certain individuals have over other individuals of the same sex and species, in exclusive relation to reproduction" (Darwin, 1871, Vol. I, p. 256). In our present view, the difference between the natural and the sexual selections is not fundamental. The selection coefficient, i.e., the difference between the Darwinian fitnesses of different genotypes, measures the relative rates of transmission of certain components of these genotypes from generation to generation. It is of lesser consequence, though certainly not immaterial, that the differential gene transmission is in some instances due to greater success in mating, while in others it is caused by differential mortality, or fertility, or greater speed of the development, or anything else. Genetic variants which are favored by the balance of all these causes will increase, and those disfavored will diminish in frequencies in the populations. Lessened success in mating may be compensated by a greater viability or fertility, or vice versa.

That sexual selection, in the classical Darwinian sense, occurs in man is clear enough. Although almost everybody in primitive societies has an opportunity to mate and produce offspring, socially more influential and more prosperous individuals may not only have access to more mates but be able to provide better conditions, which increase the probability of survival of their offspring to maturity. Good evidence of this has been provided, for example, by Salzano et al. (1967) and Chagnon et al. (1970) for Xavante and Yanomama, two of the surviving primitive tribes of South American Indians. In both tribes, as Salzano et al. say, "Whereas women are uniformly exposed to the risk of pregnancy and rarely fail to reproduce, men, on the other hand, are characterized by an appreciably higher variance in their reproductive performance." In one of the villages studied two headmen have sired approximately one-fourth of the total population.

Some forms of physiological sterility of females as well as of males are genetic. Genetic conditioning of the psychological variables which predispose individuals to spinsterhood, bachelorhood, or to prolificity in technologically advanced societies is another matter, reliable data on which are almost totally lacking. It is, for example, an open question whether homosexuality has an appreciable genetic component. However, if the existence of such genetic conditioning were proven, its bearing on race differentiation would still be in doubt. Genetically caused partial or complete sterility, better known in Drosophila than in human populations (see Marinkovic, 1967), is a part of the concealed genetic load; when the components of this load become overt, they come under control of the normalizing natural selection. Normalizing selection can hardly bring about appreciable racial differentiation. What interests us is to what extent the racial divergence of populations is brought about by directional selection, of either the sexual or the natural kind (Dobzhansky, 1970). In other words, one wishes to know not only whether a given genetic trait is influenced by selection, but also, and this is a more difficult problem, why different variants of this trait are favored in different populations. The present state of knowledge in this field is quite unsatisfactory.

Race Differences and Random Genetic Drift

The genes of the two Xavante chiefs mentioned above, who have sired about one-quarter of their village population, became more frequent in that population than the genes of the less prestigious inhabitants. Let it be noted that this is true of the genes which might facilitate access to chieftainship, as well as of genes quite irrelevant in this respect. Every chief, like any other individual, has a constellation of genes somewhat different from other chiefs or other individuals. The populations of villages containing exceptionally prolific individuals become, for that reason, genetically differentiated from one another. This has been observed among the

Xavantes and Yanomamas by the authors cited above, and by Birdsell (1972) among aboriginal Australians. Nor is such differentiation found only among primitive tribes. Glass (1954) and Steinberg et al. (1967) observed it among certain religious isolates in America; although the people involved presumably adhere to strict monogamy, variations in the numbers of children per family inevitably occur. In the course of time, these variations add up to diversification of the gene frequencies, i.e., to incipient racial diversity. In contrast to selection, which is a directional and deterministic process, here we are dealing with stochastic or random genetic processes. Random genetic drift, random walk, founder principle, and non-Darwinian evolution are some of the names applied to these processes. Can they help to explain the origin of race differences in mankind and other species? Race differences induced by natural selection have biologically a very different meaning from those induced by random genetic drift. Natural selection makes the populations differentially adapted to different environments. In other words, race differences which arose by selection are, or at some time were, adjusted to life in some kind of different circumstances. This is not necessarily the case with differences due to drift. At least initially, the populations may be adaptively equivalent. To be sure, the selection may act on the originally neutral differences and make them parts of adaptively integrated hereditary endowments. Selection and drift may in the course of evolution be interrelated.

The importance ascribed to stochastic versus deterministic processes in evolution has undergone an interesting cycle. It would be out of place to discuss the matter here in detail, but a brief account is in order. The prestige of natural selection as an evolutionary agent was at its lowest ebb during the early part of the current century, while genetics was groping for formulation of its basic concepts. Between 1926 and 1932, Chetverikov, Fisher, Haldane, and Wright arrived, largely independently, at the biological, or synthetic, theory of evolution, in which the deterministic processes are regarded as fundamental. However, Wright also recognized the importance of random genetic drift, sometimes called "the Sewall Wright principle." He did not, as he was erroneously accused by some writers, regard this principle as an alternative to or a substitute for natural selection, but as an agency, the interactions of which with natural selection have important evolutionary consequences.

Some authors, mostly nongeneticists, sought to utilize random genetic drift as an explanation of the origin of all kinds of differences between organisms to which they could not readily attribute survival value. Race differences in man are in this category. Heuristically, this was a tactical error. To investigate the effects of a trait on the Darwinian fitness of its carriers, it is more expedient to entertain as a working hypothesis that this trait may have such effects. A reaction against this error was strong in the forties, fifties, and the early sixties. Although the theoretical possibility of random drift could not be denied, its role in natural populations, and hence in evolution, was declared negligible. The pendulum has now swung back. King and Jukes (1969) published their provocative paper on non-Darwinian evolution, and Kimura and Crow (1969) and Kimura and Ohta (1969) have for quite different reasons urged that most mutational changes have no effects on fitness, and hence must be engaged in random walk in the population gene pool. Non-Darwinian evolution is now rather in fashion, especially among molecular biologists.

King and Jukes named their theory non-Darwinian because it postulates that many, if not most, evolutionary changes are not the products of natural selection. This name disregards more than a century and a half of the history of biology, which saw several non-Darwinian, i.e., nonselectionist, theories of evolution. To mention some of them: the Lamarckisms of Lamarck and of the turn-of-the-century Lamarckians (which are not the same theory), orthogenesis of Eimer, nomogenesis of Berg, aristogenesis of Osborn, as well as several frankly vitalistic notions. Darwin was himself in part a non-Darwinian, since he credited (mistakenly, we believe) the inheritance of acquired modifications as an important adjunct to natural selection. Moreover, in the *Origin of Species* he wrote: "Variations neither useful nor injurious would not be affected by natural selection, and would be left a fluctuating element, as perhaps we see in the species called polymorphic." This is as good an anticipation of the modern non-Darwinism as could be imagined.

What are the arguments in favor of the random walk being an important source of evolutionary changes? Briefly, King and Jukes argue that because of the degeneracy (redundancy) of the genetic code, about a quarter of the base substitutions in the DNA-RNA chains will give the same amino acid, and thus leave the protein coded by the gene unchanged. The relative frequencies of the 20 amino acids in diverse proteins of diverse organisms agree, with a conspicuous exception of arginine, with the statistical expectation based on the assumption of random permutations of the nucleotides in DNA. Comparison of homologous proteins in different organisms shows different numbers of amino acid substitutions, the numbers being allegedly proportional to the time elapsed since the separation of the phyletic lines leading to the organisms compared in paleontological history. This is interpreted to signify that the amino acid and nucleotide substitutions occur at uniform rates in time, as might be expected if they occurred at random, not under control of natural selection.

Unfortunately for this theory, the rates of changes are distinctly different for different proteins; some proteins conserve their amino acid sequences more tenaciously than others. This may mean that the nucleotide sequences in some genes are inherently more mutable than in others. Far more plausible is that natural selection discriminates rigorously against most changes in some genes, but is more permissive with other genes. More detailed comparisons of homologous proteins, such as cytochromes-c or hemoglobins, show that some parts of the molecules are constant in quite diverse organisms, presumably because they are essential for whatever physiological functions these proteins perform. Interesting attempts have been made to fit the numbers of changes in other parts of the same molecules to expectations based on the Poisson series, i.e., on the assumption that these changes are fixed at random, uncontrolled by natural selection. The results have been interpreted as confirming the hypothesis of random fixation, but the possibility that they are due to selection has not, in my opinion, been ruled out. There may be all degrees of likelihood that the substitutions of the amino acids at different positions will be accepted and promoted by natural selection. Since changes that obviously do not fit the Poisson series are deliberately left out of consideration, the fit of the remainder may be spurious.

Gene changes which are perceived as racial characteristics are obviously those which produce at least some visible, phenotypically detectable effects. Changes that do not alter the gene products are scarcely relevant to the present issue, however interesting they may be in other contexts. Of course, some phenotypically detectable changes may also be neutral with respect to fitness, and will represent the "fluctuating element" postulated by Darwin. Their frequencies will then be subject to random genetic drift. Given very long time and many generations, some of the changes will be lost in some populations, fixed in others, and remain fluctuating in still others. The question is whether the time intervals which must be assumed are not prohibitively long. Kimura and Ohta (1969) have shown that the average number of generations intervening between the origin and fixation of an adaptively neutral mutant gene is close to $4N_e$, where N_e is the genetically effective population size.

To evaluate the possibility that random genetic drift may have been responsible for racial differences, one would need to know at least the orders of magnitude of the N_es at different stages of human evolution. Reliable data are unfortunately lacking. Hordes, tribes, clans, and even nations may well have suffered reductions to small numbers of individuals owing to starvation, epidemics, warfare, and other calamities, and then expanded again when circumstances became propitious. A tribe may undergo fission, or give rise to small groups who move off and found a new tribe of their own. The absolute as well as effective sizes of the founder populations may be of the order of tens or even fewer. The founder variety of the genetic drift (i.e., unique or repeated reductions, rather than continuously small effective populations) may well be responsible for the intertribal genetic differences, examples of which have already been given.

That the 9 major, or for that matter the 32 local, races in Garn's classification could have arisen through the operation of the founder principle seems unlikely. Although all-or-none differences between human races are few, gene frequency differences are often considerable, and, more important, involve many genes. Even if the Amerindian, Asiatic, European, African, and other races were supposed to have descended from single pairs of progenitors, these racial Adams and Eves could not have been sampled from the same population.

The genetic divergence of the races must have been a gradual process, inasmuch as the developing races lived on different continents and under different environments, natural selection had ample opportunities to promote genes which fitted the human populations to different conditions of life. How much differentiation in neutral genetic traits could have occurred at that stage? The effective populations of the primordial races must have been in hundreds of thousands or in millions, and the average length of a generation hardly less than 20 years. The time intervening between the origin and fixation of a neutral genetic variant would then be $80N_e$, in millions or tens of millions of years. Any gene exchange between the diverging races would greatly lengthen the time, or make it infinite. These are, as indicated above, time estimates from the origin of a genetic variant to its fixation in a population. If races differ merely in the relative frequencies of certain gene alleles, neutral with respect to fitness, such differences might arise more rapidly.

Are Races of Man Genetically Adapted to Different Ways of Life?

The species mankind, in common with many, perhaps a majority of, animal and plant species, is genetically differentiated into major races (subspecies), minor races, and local populations of various orders. Because man is the only animal species having culture, certain kinds of differentiation are peculiar to him—linguistic, religious, and socioeconomic isolates, some of which may not be genetically identical. As pointed out above, most or all of this genetic differentiation is quantitative rather than qualitative. Racially distinct populations of *Homo sapiens* usually differ in frequencies of variable genes, rather than one race having 100 percent of a gene variant which another race lacks altogether. The genetic differences between human races can therefore be said to be relatively minor; in many species of animals the races have diverged genetically much further, and are on the threshold of becoming derived independent species.

All men are genetically "brothers under the skin." It is nevertheless legitimate to inquire to what extent genetic differences between populations are reflected in their health, environmental preferences, and capacity for mental development and for becoming members of different cultures. What is the biological, evolutionary function of race formation in the living world as a whole? It is differential adaptedness of subdivisions of a species for living in different geographic and ecological circumstances. Does this apply to human races? We have discussed the roles of natural selection and of random genetic drift in the origination of race differences. Differences induced by selection make the population adaptively different in some respects, at least where and when the selective process operates. The random drift may, as a first approximation, be regarded as "noise" in evolutionary adaptive processes. It is most likely that race differentiation in man arose neither by selection nor by drift alone, but by interaction of these evolutionary forces. It would nevertheless be foolhardy to attempt to dichotomize racial differences into adaptively meaningful and adaptively neutral ones.

The possibility must be considered that genetic differences between the races and populations were adaptive in the past but are neutral at present. They may have been induced by natural selection in response to the environments in which the populations lived. But human environments change radically because of the adoption of different ways of life, particularly because of cultural and technological innovations. The selection may act in a different way, or may no longer be effective in changed environments. The skin color differences are a case in point. As shown above, it is most probable that skin pigmentation was adjusted by natural selection to the climatic characteristics of the territories in which the human races were formed. But how much adaptive importance does the skin pigmentation have at present, when most people have most of their body surfaces covered with clothes, and live in artificial dwellings rather than outdoors? It may well be that for most people skin pigmentation is now an adaptively neutral characteristic.

Other examples of changing selection pressures may be found among genetic defenses against infectious diseases. Such genetic defenses became racial traits in territories in which a given infectious disease is pandemic. A classical example is the gene for the sickle red blood cell condition (hemoglobin S). Though this gene results in fatal anemia when homozygous, the heterozygous carriers not only survive but are relatively protected against some tropical forms of malarial fevers. The gene is absent in countries where these fevers do not occur, but reaches high frequencies (up to 30 percent) in some populations of tropical Africa exposed to malarial infections. Here, then, is a racial trait which was maintained by natural selection as an aid for survival in malarial environments. With malaria brought under control and perhaps approaching eradication, the S gene has lost its adaptive function. Of course, no population was ever homozygous for this gene, since it is lethal when homozygous; in the absence of malaria it is at best neutral, or mildly deleterious, when heterozygous. Its frequencies are dwindling, and it may eventually be eliminated altogether.

By far the greatest attention, and also some violent emotional reactions, are aroused by studies on possible race differences in mental traits, especially in the so-called "intelligence." Are people of all racial stocks born equal, or are some intrinsically superior and others inferior? In the first chapter of this book arguments have been presented to show that the emotional reactions unleashed by studies on the "intelligence" of human races are due to sheer misunderstanding. We need only reiterate the highlights of these arguments. Equality should not be confused with biological identity, or genetic diversity with inequality. Human equality and inequality are not statements of observable biological conditions. They are policies adopted by societies, ethical principles, and religious commandments.

People can be made equal before the law, equality of opportunity may be promoted or guaranteed, human dignity equally recognized, and human beings can be regarded equally God's sons and daughters. To be equal, people need not be identical twins, i.e., need not be genetically alike. And vice versa, regardless of how similar or different they are genetically, individuals can be treated unequally, as social superiors and inferiors, masters and servants, aristocrats and plebeians. There is no reason why monozygotic twins must necessarily be social equals, even though they are genetically as nearly identical as two individuals can be. People can be made equal or unequal by the societies in which they live; they cannot be made genetically or biologically identical, even if this were desirable. In principle, human diversity is as compatible with equality as it is with inequality.

Any two human individuals, identical twins excepted, carry different sets of genes. This has traditionally been stressed by partisans of social inequalities, and deemphasized by champions of equality. It should be the reverse—equality is meaningful only because people are not identical. Like illness, genetic lottery is no respecter of the social position or rank of the parents. Owing to gene recombination in the progeny of highly heterozygous individuals, genetically well- and poorly-endowed children are born to parents of either kind. This does not deny the existence of some positive correlations between the genetic endowments of parents and offspring. The fact that these correlations are far from complete is, however, socially and ethically no less important than that the correlations are there.

The above is a necessary preamble to the substantive

issue: Is there incontrovertible evidence of genetic differences between human populations, such as major and minor races, in mental traits, particularly in their capacities for intellectual development? The literature of the subject is as formidable in bulk as it is uncritical and unreliable. Most of it deals with ostensibly a single trait, the IQ, which in reality is a compound of several abilities that may well be genetically independent in various degrees. Furthermore, only a small minority of racial stocks have been studied, perhaps because of insuperable difficulties of devising intelligence tests that would be applicable to people speaking different languages and brought up in different cultural traditions. Whether such culture-free, or culture-fair, tests can be constructed is an open question, but it is certain that existing ones fall short of this desideratum in various degrees. There is always a danger that the tests will be biased in favor of the race, social class, culture, and subculture to which the test constructors themselves belong. A fair comparison becomes less and less possible as the groups tested differ more and more in socioeconomic, linguistic, traditional, and attitudinal backgrounds. Attempts have been made to correct for these sources of error, but with scant success.

By far the greatest number of studies deal with only two population groups—the blacks and the whites in the United States. The so-called Coleman Report (1966) is exceptional in also including IQ statistics for American Indians, Puerto Ricans, Mexican-Americans, and Oriental populations living in the United States. The plethora of papers comparing the IQ test results of whites and blacks have been uncritically compiled by Shuey (1966), and analyzed by Jensen (1969). There is no doubt that the average IQ scores of the blacks tend to be lower than those of the whites. The means for either race vary in different parts of the country, obviously depending on the socioeconomic and educational opportunities of the inhabitants of different states. In some northern states the blacks have shown higher mean scores than the whites in some southern states. However, most often the black mean is found to be 10 to 20 IQ points below the white. Jensen takes 15 points as a fair estimate of the average difference. It happens that the standard deviation (square root of variance) for the white populations is also close to 15 points. Of course, the black and white distributions overlap, and about 15 percent of the individual blacks score above the white average, while many whites score below the black average. According to the Coleman Report, the American Indians, Puerto Ricans, and Mexican-Americans are intermediate between blacks and whites, and Orientals are about equal to whites in the mean IQ score (the amount of data concerning these "ethnic" populations is a small fraction of those for the blacks and whites).

The key problem is, of course, whence comes the observed difference between the IQ means for blacks and whites? This problem has provoked ample polemics, which show no sign of subsiding. As shown in the first chapter of this book, differences in IQ scores between individuals within a population have an impressively high heritability, estimated by Jensen to be about 0.8 (80 percent). Racists have seized upon this figure as evidence of racial superiorities and inferiorities, arguing that since the heritability of the IQ variations is so high, differences in the IQ averages between races are fixed and irremediable. This is certainly unproven and unconvincing.

Jensen (1969) is fully aware of the fact that a heritability estimate for *intra*populational veriability does not necessarily tell us anything about the magnitude of the genetic component in an *inter*populational difference of means. Environments in which the racial groups live in the same country or state are appreciably and often drastically different. Even if the intrapopulational heritability were 100 percent, the interracial differences could be wholly environmental. Nevertheless Jensen argues, and rightly in my opinion, that it is not valid to attribute the interracial differences in IQ averages to undefinable differences between environments. For interpopulational, as well as for intrapopulational, differences in mean IQs, one should be able to specify just what environmental factors produce a specific effect. He appeals to studies which have tried to equate the environments of the blacks and the whites by comparing population samples of ostensibly equal socioeconomic status. When this is done, the IQ average differences diminish but do not disappear entirely. Jensen takes this as evidence of a strong genetic component in the differences between the black and white populations.

Bodmer and Cavalli-Sforza (1970), among others, have pointed out the inadequacies of equalization of the socioeconomic status as a way toward equating the total environments in which the races live. In their words:

It is difficult to see, however, how the status of blacks and whites can be compared. The very existence of a racial stratification correlated with a relative socioeconomic deprivation makes this comparison suspect. Black schools are well known to be generally less adequate than white schools, so that equal numbers of years of schooling certainly do not mean equal educational attainments. Wide variation in the level of occupation must exist within each occupational class. Thus one would certainly expect, even for equivalent occupational classes, that the black level is on the average lower than the white. No amount of money can buy a black person's way into a privileged upper-class white community, or buy off more than 200 years of accumulated racial prejudice on the part of the whites, or reconstitute the disrupted black family, in part culturally inherited from the days of slavery. It is impossible to accept the idea that matching for status provides an adequate, or even substantial, control over most important environmental differences between black and white.

One can only conclude that the degree to which differences in the IQ arrays between races are genetically conditioned is at present an unsolved problem. I fully agree with Bodmer and Cavalli-Sforza that "we do not by any means exclude the possibility that there could be a genetic component in the mean difference in IQ between races. We simply maintain that currently available data are inadequate to resolve this question in either direction." Assume for the sake of argument that some part of the average difference between the IQs of the blacks and the whites is genetic. Would it follow that the blacks are an inferior and the whites a superior race? Would it be a vindication of the racists in Alabama, South Africa, and elsewhere? Certainly not. Two basic facts refute the racists: the broad overlap of the variation curves for IQs and other human abilities, and the universal educability, and hence capacity for improvement, however that be defined.

We may accordingly agree with Darwin (1871), that "Although the existing races of man differ in many respects . . . yet if their whole organization be taken into consideration they are found to resemble each other closely in a multitude of points. . . . The same remark holds good with equal or greater force with respect to the numerous points of mental similarity between the most distinct races of man. The American aborigines, negroes and Europeans differ as much from each other in mind as any three races that can be named; yet I was incessantly struck, whilst living with the Fuegians on board the 'Beagle,' with the many little traits of character, shewing how similar their minds were to ours; and so it was with a full-blooded negro with whom I happened once to be intimate."

Races of Man and Breeds of Domestic Animals

In conclusion, consideration must be given to the argument which is the more misleading since it is superficially so plausible. Races of animal and plant species, of free-living as well as domesticated forms, develop differential adaptedness to the environments in which they live, or to the employments for which they are used. In particular, breeds of domestic animals differ, often quite strikingly, in their structural as well as behavioral characteristics.

Consider the numerous and diverse breeds of dogs, many of them specialized for different uses, with behaviors suitable for their employment. Thus shepherd dogs learn to herd sheep and cattle, scent hounds and bird dogs to find game, hunting dogs are used for pursuit, terriers for attack, and toy and lap dogs for companionship with humans. There is no doubt that these very different forms of behavior are genetically conditioned, although at the same time not only dogs but even wolves, which are their wild ancestors, possess the potentiality of being trained in different ways and of changing their behaviors accordingly (Scott and Fuller, 1965; Scott, 1968; Woolpy and Ginsburg, 1967). If the behavior of dog breeds and of breeds of other domesticated species is very strongly conditioned, why would man's races not follow this rule of genetic conditioning? Even some eminent geneticists who should have known better have been led astray by such reasoning (e.g., Darlington, 1969, 1972). Modern technologically advanced societies have been invented and built by a minority of human breeds. It is likely that the "lesser" breeds do not possess genetic aptitudes sufficient not only to create and manage but even to be members of these advanced societies.

The above argument is fallacious because it fails to take into consideration the unique and basic characteristic of human evolution (Dobzhansky, 1962, 1972). The cardinal distinction between mankind and all other forms of life is that man's adaptedness depends primarily on his cultural rather than on his genetic inheritance. Culture is acquired by each individual through learning, and is transmitted by instruction, chiefly, though not exclusively, by means of a language consisting of socially agreed-upon symbols. To adapt to new environments, mankind changes mainly its cultural inheritance, rather than its genes, as other organisms do. Of course, genes and culture are not independent but interdependent. It is man's genetic endowment which makes him able to think in symbols, abstractions, and generalizations. The potentiality of cultural evolution, which is uniquely human, has developed through the evolution of his gene pool. But the contents of his gene pool do not determine the contents of his culture. By way of analogy, genes give man his ability to speak, but do not decide just what he shall say on a given occasion.

The basic, and unique, capacity of man is his genetically established educability by means of symbolic language. This educability is a species trait common to all races and all nonpathological individuals. Its universality is no more surprising than that all people have body temperature and the pH of the blood varying only within narrow limits. Both educability and symbolic language became universal human traits because survival and success in man-made environments depended on possession of these traits. Nothing of the sort happened in any other wild or domesticated animal species. By contrast, genetically fixed specializations in both body structure and behavior have often been deliberately built into different domestic breeds.

In sum: breeds of domestic animals often differ in behavior, and the differences are genetically more or less rigidly fixed. Their behavior is a part of the complex of characteristics which make a given breed suitable for performance of a certain kind of work or function. The kind of behavior exhibited, as well as its degree of fixity, are induced by the artificial selection which the owners or masters of the animals practiced, deliberately or unwittingly, in the process of formation of a given breed. The evolutionary pattern of the human species is quite different. Natural selection has unrelentingly favored the ability of human beings to learn and to modify their behavior depending on the circumstances of their upbringing and social conditions in the midst of which they find themselves. This is precisely the opposite of selection in breeds of domesticated animals. Furthermore, selection for trainability and cultural receptivity has been going on not in some populations and races but in the whole human species, and uninterruptedly ever since the inception of humanity and of its dependence on culture as a method of adaptation to and control of the environment. Two million years and 100 thousand generations are probably conservative estimates of the duration of this selective process. The evolutionary uniqueness of the human species should not be underestimated.

⚜ 3 ⚜

EPILOGUE:

MAN'S IMAGE

ABOUT THREE CENTURIES AGO, Pascal described the human condition with a lucidity and poignancy never since equaled:

When I consider the short duration of my life, swallowed up in the eternity before and after, the little space which I fill, and even can see, engulfed in the infinite immensity of spaces of which I am ignorant and which knew me not, I am frightened, and am astonished at being here rather than there; for there is no reason why here rather than there, why now rather than then. Who has put me here? By whose order and direction have this

From Ben Rothblatt, ed., *Changing Perspectives of Man* (Chicago: University of Chicago Press, 1968), pp. 175–190. Reprinted by permission.

place and this time been allotted to me? The eternal silence of these infinite spaces frightens me.

Whether the silence of the infinite spaces is more or less frightening to our contemporaries than it was to Pascal is hard to tell. The spaces still know us not, but we begin to know something about the spaces. By whose order this place and time have been allotted to us has, however, become, if anything, still more mysterious.

Objects most remote from us yet discovered in the universe are galaxies some five billion light-years away. The mysterious quasars (quasi-stellar objects), or some of them, may be as remote, but their nature and remoteness are still under dispute among cosmologists. This is a remoteness which staggers the imagination; the radiation from these objects reaching us today left its source billions of years ago. The universe is believed to have started in a cosmic explosion which made the universe "expand," or rather caused its different components to fly apart in all directions with colossal speeds. The date of this explosion, and consequently the supposed age of the universe, is estimated to be on the order of 10 to 15 billion years. These estimates tend, however, to be lengthened rather than shortened by newer discoveries.

The number of galaxies in the universe visible in the 200-inch telescope is estimated to be close to one billion. Our galaxy is merely one of these, yet it may contain between one million and 100 million planetary systems. One of these includes a medium-sized planet which we inhabit. The supposition that the planet earth is in any way unique or exceptional or privileged seems far-fetched to many scientists. It is, however, the only one known for certain to have a tiny proportion of its mass involved in a process called life. Moreover, the diversity of living beings is very impressive. There are at least two million kinds, or species, of life on earth at present, and there were more in the past, which became extinct.

The Problem of Extraterrestrial Life

Speculation is rife concerning the possibility that there may be life of some sort on other planets, in other planetary systems, and in other galaxies. Some authorities go so far as to proclaim it a certainty that life not merely could but must have arisen in many places in the universe. More than that, sentient and rational beings must have evolved on many planets where there is life. In other words, "We are not alone." The name "exobiology" has been invented for the study of the assumed extraterrestrial life. The problems of exobiology cannot be adequately discussed here; I realize that the following remarks may do injustice to the ingenious speculations advanced in this field. I cannot, however, help wondering if the exobiologists may not turn out to be high-powered specialists on a nonexistent subject. The stock argument in favor of the existence of life in many places in the universe runs about as follows: Although the critical step from the nonliving to the living may be a rare and im-probable event, there are some 100 million planets in our galaxy on which this step coud be made, hence it must have been made on several or even on many. This argument is not really convincing, however, because nobody knows for sure just how probable or improbable the event may be under various circumstances. It is certain that the event happened at least once—on earth. The evidence that it was not a unique event is yet to be obtained—it cannot be taken for granted.

Let us, however, assume for the sake of further argument that life did arise in many places, and moreover that it was life based on nucleic acids and proteins, in other words, life chemically of the same kind as that on earth. This granted, it far from follows that such life must have evolved elsewhere as it did on our planet, let alone that it must have produced humanoid organisms. Evolution is principally adaptation to the environment; however, even if the environments somewhere happened to be much like, though of course not identical with, those on earth, a reenactment or repetition of the terrestrial evolutionary history has a probability very close to zero. This is because biological evolution is not predetermined to achieve any particular form of adaptedness to the environment. It has a range of possibilities that is virtually unlimited.

Evolution is a creative process which is most unlikely to occur two or more times in the same way. Man was not contained in the primordial life, except as one of an infinitely large number of possibilities. What these other unrealized possibilities might have been we probably shall never know. And yet, the origin of man was not an accident either, unless you choose to consider all history, including biological history and that of human societies, states, and nations, as series of accidents. This is a possible view, but not an appealing one. It is far more meaningful to describe biological and human histories as successions of unique events, each event being casually related to what went on before and to what will follow in the future, and yet nonrecurrent. George Simpson (1964) gave arguments essentially similar

to the above in a brilliant chapter entitled "The Non-preva-
ence of Humanoids," that is, nonprevalence anywhere except on our planet. Our species, mankind, is almost certainly
alone in the universe, and to that extent our planet is also
unique.

To recognize this "aloneness" is not necessarily to experience the Pascalian "fright" and "astonishment." Quite the
opposite. The space which mankind fills, and the duration
of its existence so far, are indeed very small compared to the
now known "immensity of spaces." The messages that we
may wish to send describing human activities on earth may
have to travel billions of years at the speed of light to reach
the quasars and the remotest galaxies, and there is probably
nobody there to receive these messages. Does it mean that
all our doings, both those of individuals and of the human
species as a whole, are mere whiffs of insignificance? Not at
all; because it is unique, the career of the human species
here on earth may be of cosmic significance. The idea need
not be a wildly conceited delusion. Our species may well be
alone in having discovered that the universe and all that it
contains, including mankind, is a changing product of evolution. It is neither size nor geometric centrality in the solar
system, or in our galaxy, or in the universe, that makes the
planet earth so important. It is that the flames of self-aware-
ness, of death awareness, and of evolutionary awareness
have been kindled here on earth and probably nowhere else.

Evolution and Man's Image

The image of man as seen by Pascal and his contemporaries
and successors is different from that emerging from evolu-

tionary science. The difference becomes understandable when viewed against the background of the history of science and its philosophical implications since Copernicus, Galileo, Newton, and Darwin. Here again I am forced to be too brief and, I fear, too dogmatic. The pre-Copernican man felt certain not only that he was the heart of the universe but that the universe was created for him and because of him. The earth was the hub of several concentric spheres: those of the moon, the sun, the planets, and fixed stars. God watched the smallest happenings on earth from somewhere up above. The interior of the earth contained an elaborately engineered hell; a man could avoid becoming its resident in perpetuity only by good behavior during his brief sojourn on the earth's surface, and by the intercession of the properly constituted ecclesiastic authorities. With travel difficult and slow, the earth seemed to be very large. It shrank progressively as it was gradually explored and as travel became easy and rapid. It is quite small in the age of jet aircraft. But whether large or small, the earth existed for man and for the realization of God's mysterious plans for man's salvation.

All these arrangements did not make man free of anxieties. He faced the *mysterium tremendum*—why has God arranged things as he has? This was, however, just one extra mystery —the greatest one to be sure—but mysteries were all around, from the vagaries of weather to the behavior of one's friends and enemies. All these things were the doing of spirits, good or evil. Though spirits were more powerful than men, men were not entirely defenseless against them, because one could secure the assistance of some spirits against others.

The development of science changed the situation. The mystery seemed to recede, but in fact it was relegated to the beginning of the world. Copernicus, after him Kepler and Galileo, and still later Newton, together with their many followers and successors, changed the image of the universe and of man. The earth is a smallish planet revolving around a much grander sun. Instead of the celestial spheres there is only the endless void, in which other planets, suns, and galaxies are as tiny islets on an infinite ocean. Man is lost in cosmic spaces. It is not, however, the dimensional smallness of man that really matters. It is rather the mechanical and inexorably deterministic nature of the universe, and finally of man himself, that changes man's image. Celestial phenomena are calculable and predictable, provided that one has discovered the precise and eternal laws which they obey. Biological and psychological phenomena are less predictable, but only because they are much more complex and the laws governing them are yet to be discovered. Descartes decided that the human body was as much a machine as a clock or other "automation," although he still believed that man had a nonmechanical soul. Others found the hypothesis of soul to be superfluous. Man is a machine, and that is that.

God was found to be another superfluous hypothesis. To be sure, Newton and many other scientists tried to hold on to their religions. Newton thought that the planets were hurled into their paths initially by God. But subsequent to this divine act at the beginning, the planets follow their proper orbits, according to immutable laws and without further guidance. The deists thought that God was the original creator and lawgiver of the universe. Having created the universe and set it in motion, God found it so well made that his presence became no longer essential. Instead of mysteries, we have the laws of nature. Some people thought that God reserves the right of occasional miraculous intervention, temporarily abrogating the very laws which he himself has formerly established. To others, such behavior appears unseemly for the all-wise and omniscient creator. It is more convenient to imagine him as a sort of absentee landlord who lets things take their "natural" courses.

Mystery driven out through the front door tends to creep in through the back door. Has the creator and lawgiver arranged things really well? If he is credited with the order, beauty, and goodness in the world, he must by the same token be responsible for the disorder, ugliness, and evil. The machinery of the world has serious flaws, and this is a mystery defying comprehension. An absentee-landlord god can hardly be prayed to, since he is unable or unwilling to intervene to change the causal sequences which bring about events.

To this is added the hopelessness of determinism. As stated by Laplace, the doctrine of determinism is essentially that if one knew the position and speed of every particle in the universe at any single instant, and if one could submit this knowledge to analysis, one could predict all future events and also retrodict all past events. Although this statement contains two pretty vertiginous "ifs," determinism is an explicit or implicit faith which is the basis of scientific activity. It leads, however, to an embarrassing inference: there is nothing new in the world, because all that ever happens was predestined from the beginning. No human effort, or absence of effort, can change anything, because the effort or its absence is equally predestined. This is a far stronger fatalism than the fatalism sometimes (and mostly wrongly) ascribed to oriental philosophies.

Darwin has been called the Newton of biology, although the Copernicus or the Galileo of biology would perhaps be a better characterization. There is as yet nothing in biology analogous to, say, the laws of gravitation; the Newton of biology may be yet to come. To say this is not to underestimate Darwin's contribution. He has shown that the biological species, including man, have not appeared ready-made; their multifarious structures and functions are not mere whims of nature or of a creator. Every living species is a descendant of ancestors unlike itself, and generally more unlike the farther back in time one looks. It is probable, though not certain, that all beings now alive are descendants of one primordial life which appeared some four billion years ago. Presumed remains of living beings three and one-half billion years old have recently been found. The organic diversity is a consequence of adaptation to different environments; the endless variety of bodily structures and functions makes possible an endless diversity of modes of life. There are so many kinds of organisms because they can exploit more fully than any single organism conceivably could the diverse opportunities which an environment offers for living.

Evolutionary Uniqueness of Man

The human species has evolved a unique way to cope with its environments. This way is culture. Culture is not transmitted from generation to generation by the genes, although its biological basis is so transmitted. Culture has been called "superorganic," although it surely rests on an organic foundation. Man is an animal, but he is so extraordinary that he is much more than an animal. Darwin and his successor evolutionists have thus extended to the living world, and even to the human world, the principles which were shown to be supremely efficient in the study of the physical world. Biology has by now exorcised the ghost of vitalism, which wanted to see in life something radically incommensurable with the rest of nature. Mechanism has triumphed in biology. This triumph was what Darwin and the evolution theory were, and still are, mainly acclaimed for. There is, however, another aspect to evolutionism which may be at least equally and possibly more important. It sees the whole universe, and everything in it, in the process of change and development. The universe is on its way to somewhere. Where is it going?

The grandeur of the Newtonian image of the universe was in its serene constancy and the precision of its laws. Planets and their satellites follow their orbits again and again, in predictable fashion. Moreover, since Newton accepted the traditional creation date as well as the apocalyptic prediction of the end of the world, there was little opportunity for change either in the past or the future. The laws of the conservation of mass and of energy were discovered later; here was a break in the constancy, however—although energy is conserved, it undergoes a directional change because of entropy.

What biological evolution is all about, however, is not constancy but change. Darwin and his successors have shown that the living world of today is different from what it was in the past, and that it may become different again in the future. Mankind proved to have a hitherto quite unsuspected kind of history, the history of its slow emergence from its animal ancestors, in addition to the recorded history of patriarchs, kings, battles, and empires. While recorded history goes back only a few thousand years, biological history extends somewhere between one and a half and two million years. But even this history is short relative to that of the life from which man came, which took perhaps four billion years. And back of that are more billions of years, when the universe existed without either life or man.

I do not wish to be understood as claiming that it was Darwin who made evolution into a universal principle. In point of fact, it was recognized before Darwin that the planetary system has had a history of origin from the primitive sun, or from a mass of matter which gave origins both to the sun and to the planets. Human history has been studied at least since Herodotus and Thucydides; late in the eighteenth century Condorcet ascribed to it a directional character—from a primitive barbarianism to an earthly paradise of perfect enlightenment. Darwin's theory of biological evolution is, however, the keystone of the evolutionary conception of the world, beginning with the evolution of the cosmos and culminating in the evolution of mankind. Modern cosmology is evolutionary cosmology. Even the atoms of the chemical elements, hitherto symbols of indivisibility and unchangeability, proved to have had an envolutionary history. In the homely language of some modern cosmologists, the atoms were "cooked" in the explosion at the start of cosmic evolution, and are still being cooked in the furnaces of the interior of the sun and the stars.

It has been urged by some authorities that the term "evolution" should be restricted to biological evolution only. I do not share this view, because it seems to me important to convey the idea that change and development are characteristic of nonliving as well as of living matter and of human affairs. This does not prevent one from recognizing that the processes of cosmic, inorganic, or geological evolution are different from biological evolutionary processes. The causes of biological evolution must be looked for in heredity, mutation, and natural selection. None of these is found in nonliving systems, and the analogies which some authors have attempted to draw are at best remote. Other analogues of heredity, mutation, and natural selection have been claimed in human social and cultural evolution with, I fear, even less success. These analogies are more often obfuscating than enlightening.

Nor can I see much of an advantage in the views expounded so brilliantly by such philosophers as Whitehead and Hartshorn. They like to ascribe to inorganic systems, and even to atoms and subatomic particles, some rudiments of life, individuality, and, further, of consciousness and volition. It is almost needless to say that there is no positive evidence, either compelling or presumptive, of any such biological and human qualities in nonliving systems. Even as a speculative possibility these views do not seem to me attractive. They really amount to a denial of anything substantially new ever arising in evolution. They are most nearly analogous to the early performistic notions in biology; some eighteenth-century biologists believed that a sex cell contains a "homunculus," a tiny figure of man. This seemed to make the problem of development very simple—the homunculus had only to grow in size to become an adult man, and a corresponding miniature in an animal sex cell had to grow to become an adult animal of the proper species. But this simplicity was deceptive, since it made the problem of development of succeeding generations insoluble. One had to believe that homunculi contained second-order homunculi, these had third-order homunculi, and so on. An analogous difficulty arises with the "minds" of atoms. It might seem at first that human mind could simply evolve by growth of the atomic mind. Human mind is, however, somehow associated with the human brain, and where are the brains of atoms and electrons?

The most interesting aspect of evolution is precisely that it creates novelties. From time to time it transcends itself, i.e., produces novel systems with novel properties—properties which the antecedent systems did not have even as tiny germs. Emergence of the living from the nonliving and emergence of humanity from animality are the two grandest evolutionary transcendences so far. Teilhard de Chardin was the evolutionist who had the courage to predict further transcendences, mankind moving toward what he called the megasynthesis and toward Point Omega, this last being his symbol for God. Here is evidently a borderland, in which Teilhard's science has collaborated with his mystical vision. I am not planning in the present discussion to take you on an excursion in this borderland of prophecy.

As already stated, we do not know for sure whether the transcendences of the nonliving to life, and of animal to man, have taken place solely on this planet earth or in many places in the universe. Perhaps some positive information bearing on this issue will come from the progress in space travel. Be that as it may, we do have conclusive enough evidence that these three kinds of evolution—inorganic, organic, and human—have happened here on earth. These three kinds of evolution are not independent of each other; they are rather the three stages of the single evolution of the cosmos. By calling them stages, I do not mean to suggest that cosmic evolution stopped when the biological phase started, or that biological evolution stopped when the human phase began. On the contrary, the three kinds of evolution are not only going on, but are connected by feedback relations. For example, geography influences the living things which inhabit a given territory; in turn, vegetation, animals, and especially human activities have now become geographic and even geologic agents. Human cultural evolution influences mankind's genetic endowment, and vice versa. In recent years there have been publicized some alarmist views asserting that human genetic endowment is in a process of degeneration, and predicting dire consequences for the future. This matter cannot be adequately discussed in this book; I believe that the dangers have been exaggerated, and in any case the situation is not beyond possible control.

The evolutionary view of the world does not abrogate the classical Newtonian mechanistic view. The change which evolutionism makes is nevertheless of greatest importance for man's views of himself and of his place in the universe. The classical conception stressed the essential permanence of things, at least for the duration of the world's existence. The evolutionary conception emphasizes change and movement. The preevolutionary world view did not, of course, deny all change, but the changes were usually represented as cyclic, and the world as a whole did not go anywhere in particular. Spring, summer, autumn, and winter return again and again at the appointed times; people are born, grow, build families, get old, and die, and a new generation goes through the same succession of stages; plants and animals, like people, produce generation after generation; heavenly bodies follow their orbits again and again; mountains rise, are eroded away, become submerged in the sea, rise up again, and so on. But to translate a French adage, the more things change, the more they remain the same.

Constancy, lack of change, and regular recurrence seem to be reassuring and comforting to many people. "Like the good old days" is a compliment tinged with nostaliga. Change brings insecurity; one has to become adapted, adjusted, or reconciled to altered situations. Yet changelessness, or eternal repetition or return, is the acme of futility. A world which remains forever the same is senseless. It is what Dostoevsky called a "devil's vaudeville." All the strivings and struggles which a person, or a generation, has to go through are in vain because the next generation, and the one after that, and so on, ad infinitum, will have to go through the same struggles all over again.

What difference does the idea of evolution make? Quite simply, it is this: the universe is not a status but a process. Its creation was not something which happened a few thousand years ago, before any of us were born and could have influenced it in any way. The creation is going forward now, and may conceivably go on indefinitely. The view that "there is nothing new under the sun" is in error. In the past there were an earth and a sun different from the present ones, and there will be a new earth and a new sun in the future. An important role in this forward movement belongs to the phenomenon called life, and to one particular form thereof called mankind, which exists as far as we know only on a single and not otherwise remarkable planet.

Evolution as a Creative Process

The evolution of life is remarkably rapid, measured on a cosmic time scale. Ten million years ago, the oceans and mountains, the moon, the sun, and the stars were not very different from what they are now, but the living beings inhabiting the earth were rather unlike the present ones. Ten thousand years ago mankind was quite different from what it is now, while except for the destruction of some biological species, the biological world was pretty much what we now observe. Evolution is a creative process; the creativity is most pronounced in human cultural evolution, less in biological, and least in inorganic evolution.

A creative process by its very nature always risks ending in a failure or being stranded in a blind alley. Every biological species is nature's experiment, essaying a new mode of living. Most species eventually prove unsuccessful and become extinct without issue. Yet some, a minority, discover new or superior ways of getting a living out of the environment which is available on earth. These few lucky discoverers inherit the earth and undergo what is technically known as adaptive radiation. That is, the surviving species differentiate and become many species again, only to repeat the process of discovery, extinction, and new adaptive radiation. Yet this is not another specimen of eternal return. New adaptive radiations do not simply restore what there was earlier; the new crop of species may contain some which have achieved novel or surer ways of remaining alive, or have discovered previously unexploited niches in the environment and have thus augmented the living at the expense of the nonliving.

The trial-and-error process of proliferation of ever-new species and of disappearance of the old ones has achieved remarkable successes. Biological evolution has transcended itself by giving rise to man. Mankind as a species is biologically an extraordinary success. It has gained the ability to adapt its environments to its genes, as well as its genes to its environments. This ability stems from a novel, extragenetically transmitted complex of adaptive traits called culture. Culture leads to still another kind of discovery, discoveries of knowledge, which can be transmitted to succeeding generations again by means of the extragenic processes of instruction and learning. One of the discoveries which became known is the discovery of evolution. Man knows that the universe and life have evolved, and that mankind entered this universe by way of evolution. With perhaps a bit too much poetic license, it has been said that man is evolution having become conscious of itself. It is no exaggeration, however, to say that having discovered evolution, man has opened up a possibility of eventually learning how to control it.

The enterprise of creation has not been completed; it is going on before our eyes. Ours is surely not the best of all thinkable worlds, and, we hope, not even the best of all possible worlds. Man is constantly asking whether his existence, and that of the universe in which he finds himself, has any sense or meaning. If there is no evolution, then all is futility—human life in particular. If the world evolves, then hope is at least possible.

An uncomfortable question inevitably presents itself at this point. Can science ever discover meaning in anything, and is a scientist entitled even to inquire about meanings and purposes? To a rigorous mechanicist who does not wish to think in evolutionary terms, such words as meaning, improvement, progress, and transcendence are meaningless noises. Everything in the world, including myself, is an aggregation of atoms. When this aggregation disaggregates, the atoms will still be there and may aggregate into something else. Is there an objectively definable difference between an object of art and a junk heap? If a virus and a man are nothing but different seriations of the nucleotides in their DNAs and RNAs, then all of evolution was a lot of "sound and fury signifying nothing."

One of the exasperating phenomena of the intellectual history of mankind is politely called "the academic lag." This crudely mechanistic world view was acceptable in science chiefly during the eighteenth and nineteenth centuries. It had justified itself by having given a powerful impetus to scientific discovery. It is now being displaced by the evolutionary world view. Yet the representatives of what C. P. Snow has referred to as literary or nonscientific culture have only recently discovered that the world is nothing but an aggregation of atoms. It is a curious experience to hear an artist argue that a junk heap is, indeed, no less worthy of aesthetic appreciation than is the "Venus de Milo," because both are matter wrought into arbitrary shapes; or to have an eminent musician declare that the atonality and certain other characteristics of avant-garde music are merely recognition of the Copernican discovery that man is not the center of the universe; or to read in a book by an intellectual pundit that "something pervasive that makes the difference, not between civilized man and the savage, not between man and the animals, but between man and the robot, grows numb, ossifies, falls away like black mortified flesh when techne assails the senses and science dominates the mind."

In reality, science is neither a villain debasing human dignity nor the sole source of human wisdom. In Toynbee's words:

Science's horizon is limited by the bounds of Nature, the ideologies' horizon by the bounds of human social life, but the human soul's range cannot be confined within either of these limits. Man is a bread-eating social animal, but he is also something more. He is a person, endowed with a conscience and a will, as well as with a self-conscious intellect. This spiritual endowment of his condemns him to a life-long struggle to reconcile himself with the Universe into which he has been born.

The fact that the universe was evolved and is evolving is surely relevant to this reconciliation. The advent of evolutionism makes it necessary to ask a new question which simply could not occur to those who believed that the world is created once and for all, stable and changeless.

The question is: Where is evolution going? This question can be asked separately about the three known kinds of evolution—cosmic, biological, and human. It has also been asked about evolution as a whole, because the three kinds of evolution can be viewed as the constituent parts, or stages, of a single all-embracing process of universal evolution. This universe, so formidable and so beautiful, is in a process of change. It may be that evolution is merely drifting at random, and going nowhere in particular. There is, however, also a possibility, for which no rigorous demonstration can be given, that universal evolution is one grand enterprise in which everything and everybody are component parts. Whose enterprise is this, and with what aim and for what purpose is it undertaken? The four centuries of the growth of science since Copernicus have not dispelled this mystery; the one century since Darwin has made it more urgent than ever.

What role is man to play in evolution? Is he to be a mere spectator or, perchance, the spearhead and eventual director? There are people who will shrug this question off, or recoil from it, considering it an exhibition of insane arrogance. Since, however, man is one and presumably the only rational being who has become aware that evolution is happening, he can hardly avoid asking such questions. The issue involved is no less than the meaning of his own existence. Does man live just to live, and is there no more sense or meaning to him than that? Or is he called upon to participate in the construction of the best thinkable universe?

BIBLIOGRAPHY

Allard, R. W.; and Kannenberg, L. W. 1968. Population studies in predominantly self-pollinating species. *Evolution* 22: 517–528.

Anastasi, A. 1958. *Differential psychology.* New York: Macmillan.

Baker, P. T.; Buskirk, E. R.; Kollias, J.; and Mazess, R. B. 1967. Temperature regulation at high altitude: Quechua Indians and U.S. whites during total body cold exposure. *Human Biol.* 39:155–169.

Baker, P. T.; and Weiner, J. 1966. *Biology of human adaptability.* Oxford: Oxford University Press.

Bielicki, T. 1962. Some possibilities for estimating interpopulation relationship on the basis of continuous traits. *Current Anthrop.* 3:3–8.

Birdsell, J. B. 1972. *Human evolution.* Chicago: Rand McNally.

Bodmer, W. F.; and Cavalli-Sforza, L. L. 1970. Intelligence and race. *Sci. American* 223:19–29.

Bose, N. K. 1951. Caste in India. *Man in India* 31:107–123.

Boyd, W. C. 1950. *Genetics and the races of man.* Boston: Little, Brown.

Brown, R. 1965. *Social psychology.* New York: Free Press.

Burt, C. 1961. Intelligence and social mobility. *Brit. J. Stat. Psychol.* 14:3–24.

Butcher, H. J. 1968. *Human intelligence.* London: Methuen.

Cavalli-Sforza, L. L. 1959. Some data on the genetic structure of human populations. *Proc. X Internat. Congr. Genetics* 1:389–407.

———. 1969. Human diversity. *Proc. XII Internat. Congr. Genetics* 3:405–416.

———; and Bodmer, W. F. 1971. *The genetics of human populations.* San Francisco: Freeman.

Chagnon, N. A.; Neel, J. V.; Weitkamp, L.; Gershowitz, H.; and Ayres, M. 1970. The influence of cultural factors on the demography and pattern of gene flow from the Makiritare to the Yanomama Indians. *Amer. J. Phys. Anthrop.* 32:339–350.

Coleman, J. S. 1966. *Equality of educational opportunity.* Washington, D.C.: U.S. Office of Education.

Czekanowski, J. 1962. The theoretical assumptions of Polish anthropology. *Current Anthrop.* 3:481–494.

Darlington C. D. 1969. The evolution of man and society. London: Allen and Unwin.

———. 1972. Race, class, and culture. In J. W. S. Pringle, ed., *Biology and the human sciences.* 95–120. Oxford: Clarendon Press.

Darwin, C. 1871. *The descent of man, and selection in relation to sex.* 2 vol. London: John Murray.

Dobzhansky, T. 1962. *Mankind evolving.* New Haven: Yale University Press.

———. 1964. *Heredity and the nature of man.* New York: Harcourt Brace Jovanovich.

———. 1970. *Genetics of the evolutionary process.* New York: Columbia University Press.

———. 1972. Unique aspects of human evolution. In J. W. S. Pringle, ed., *Biology and the human sciences.* Oxford: Clarendon Press.

Eckland, B. K. 1967. Genetics and sociology: A reconsideration. *Amer. Sociol. Rev.* 32:173–194.

———. 1970. New mating boundaries in education. *Social Biol.* 17:269–277.

———. 1971. Social class structure and the genetic basis of intelligence. In R. Cancro, ed., *Intelligence.* 65–76. New York: Grune & Stratton.

———. 1972a. Evolutionary consequences of differential fertility and assortative mating in man. *Evol. Biol.* 5:293–305.

———. 1972b. Trends in the direction and intensity of natural selection, with special reference to the effects of destratification and equal opportunity upon current birth rates. Paper read at the American Museum of Natural History—American Eugenics Society Symposium on Human Evolution, November 18–20, 1971, New York.

———. Population genetics and evolutional selection in the U.S.A. Chapter to appear in H. V. Munsham, ed., *Education and population.* In press.

Erlenmeyer-Kimling, L.; and Jarvik, L. F. 1963. Genetics and intelligence, a review. *Science* 142:1477–1479.

Eysenck, H. J. 1971. *Race, intelligence and education.* New York: Library Press.

Fried, M. H. 1968. The need to end the pseudoscientific investigation of race. In M. Mead, T. Dobzhansky, E. Tobach, and R. E. Light, eds., *Science and the concept of race.* New York: Columbia University Press.

Garn, S. M. 1965. *Human races.* Springfield: Charles Thomas.

Glass, B. 1954. Genetic changes in human populations, especially those due to gene flow and genetic drift. *Adv. Genetics* 6:95–139.

Gottesman, I. I. 1968a. A sampler of human behavior genetics. *Evol. Biol.* 2:276–320.

————. 1968b. Biogenetics of race and class. In M. Deutsch, I. Katz, and A. R. Jensen, eds., *Social class, race, and psychological development.* 11–50. New York: Holt, Rinehart and Winston.

Hamilton, W. J.; and Heppner, F. 1967. Radiant solar energy and the function of black homeotherm pigmentation; an hypothesis. *Science* 155:196–197.

Harris, H. 1967. Enzyme variation in man: Some general aspects. *Proc. III Internat. Congr. Human Genetics* 207–214.

Harrison, G. A. 1967. Human evolution and ecology. *Proc. III Internat. Congr. Human Genetics* 351–359.

Heber, R. 1968. *Rehabilitation of families at risk for mental retardation.* Madison: University of Wisconsin Regional Rehabilitation Center.

Herrnstein, R. 1971. I.Q. *Atlantic Monthly* 43–64.

Jensen, A. R. 1969. How much can we boost IQ and scholastic achievement? *Harvard Educ. Rev.* 31:1–123.

King, J. L.; and Jukes, T. H. 1969. Non-Darwinian evolution. *Science* 164:788–798.

Kimura, M.; and Crow, J. F. 1969. Natural selection and gene substitution. *Gen. Research* 13:127–141.

Kimura, M.; and Ohta, T. 1969. The average number of generations until fixation of a mutant gene in a finite population. *Genetics* 61:763–771.

Lerner, I. M. 1954. *Genetic homeostasis.* Edinburgh: Oliver & Boyd.

Lewontin, R. C.; and Hubby, J. L. 1966. A molecular approach to the study of genetic heterozygosity in natural poulations. II. *Genetics* 54:595–609.

Lipset, S. M. 1968. Social class. *Internat. Encycl. Soc. Sciences* 15:296–316.

Lundman, B. 1967. *Geographische anthropologie.* Stuttgart: Gustav Fischer.

Malia, M. E. 1972. The intellectuals, adversaries or clerisy? *Daedalus* Summer 1972:206–216.

Marinkovic, D. 1967. Genetic loads affecting fertility in natural populations of *Drosophila pseudoobscura. Genetics* 57:701–709.

Mayr, E. 1963. *Animal species and evolution*. Cambridge: Belknap.

Mourant, A. E. 1954. *The distribution of human blood groups*. Oxford: Blackwell.

———; Kopec, A. C., and Domaniewska Sobczak, K. 1958. *The ABO blood groups: Comprehensive tables and maps of world distribution*. Oxford: Blackwell.

Myrdal, G. 1962. *An American dilemma*. New York: Harper & Row.

Neel, J. V. 1969. Some changing constraints on the human evolutionary process. *Proc. XII Internat. Congr. Genetics* 3:389–403.

Newman, M. T. 1963. Geographic and microgeographic races. *Current Anthropol.* 4:189–191, 204–205.

Osborn, F. 1968. *The future of human heredity*. New York: Weybright & Talley.

Otten, C. M. 1967. On pestilence, diet, natural selection, and the distribution of microbial and human blood group antigens and antibodies. *Current Anthropol.* 8:209–226.

Prakash, S.; and Lewontin, R. C. 1968. A molecular approach to the study of heterozygosity in natural populations. III. *Proc. Nat. Acad. Sci.* 59:398–405.

Putnam, C. 1967. *Race and reality*. Washington, D.C.: Public Affairs Press.

Riggs, S. K.; and Sargent, F. 1964. Physiological regulation in moist heat by young American Negro and white males. *Human Biol.* 36:339–353.

Salzano, F. M.; Neel, J. V.; and Maybury-Lewis, D. 1967. Further studies on the Xavante Indians. *Amer. J. Human Genetics* 19:463–489.

Scarr-Salapatek, S. 1971a. Unknowns in the IQ equation. (Review.) *Science* 174:1223–1228.

———. 1971b. Race, social class, and IQ. *Science* 174:1285–1295.

Scott, J. P. 1968. Evolution and domestication of the dog. *Evol. Biol.* 2:243–275.

———; and Fuller, J. L. 1965. *Genetics and the social behavior of the dog*. Chicago: University of Chicago Press.

Shields, J. 1962. *Monozygotic twins brought up apart and brought up together.* London: Oxford University Press.

Shuey, A. M. 1966. *The testing of Negro intelligence.* New York: Social Science Press.

Simpson, G. 1964. *This view of life.* New York: Harcourt, Brace, and World.

Singer, E.; and Galston, A. W. 1972. Education and science in China. *Science* 175:15–22.

Skodak, M.; and Skeels, H. M. 1949. A final follow-up study of one hundred adopted children. *J. Genet. Psychol.* 75: 85–128.

Spuhler, J. N., and Lindzey, G. 1967. Racial differences in behavior. In J. Hirsch, ed., *Behavior—genetic analysis.* 366–414. New York: McGraw-Hill.

Steinberg, A. G.; Bleibtreu, H. K.; Kurczynski, T. W.; Martin, A. O.; and Kurczynski, A. M. 1967. Genetic studies in an inbred human isolate. *Proc. III Internat. Congr. Human Genetics* 267–289.

Thomson, W. R. 1967. Some problems in the genetic study of personality and intelligence. In J. Hirsch, ed., *Behavior—genetic analysis.* 344–365. New York: McGraw-Hill.

Toynbee, A. 1956. *An historian's approach to religion.* London: Oxford University Press.

————. 1961. *A study of history.* 12 Vols. London: Oxford University Press.

Tyler, L. E. 1965. *The psychology of human differences.* New York: Appleton-Century-Crofts.

Vandenberg, S. G. 1970. A comparison of heritability estimates of U.S. Negro and white high school students. *Acta Genet. Med. Gemel.* 19:280–284.

Wallace, B. 1968. *Topics in population genetics.* New York: Norton.

Wiercinski, A. 1962. The racial analysis of human populations in relation to their ethnogenesis. *Current Anthropol.* 3:2, 9–20.

Woolpy, J. H.; and Ginsburg, B. E. 1967. Wolf socialization, a study of temperament in a wild social species. *Amer. Zoologist* 7:357–363.

Wright, S. 1969. *Evolution and the genetics of populations. The theory of gene frequencies.* Chicago: University of Chicago Press.

INDEX

THE AUTHOR

THEODOSIUS DOBZHANSKY is one of the world's foremost geneticists. His achievements have been recognized by universities and national science academies all over the world. He has always been concerned to make his scientific interests serve the existence and destiny of humankind. This concern is reflected in the titles of his major books, including *Evolution, Genetics and Man; The Biological Basis of Human Freedom; Mankind Evolving; The Biology of Ultimate Concern;* and *Genetics of the Evolutionary Process.* Today, at the age of 73, he is Professor Emeritus at Rockefeller University and is continuing his researches as an Adjunct Professor at the University of California, Davis.